A Definitive Handbook for Learning and Playing Well the Game of "42"

J. Ronald Adair

Published by

ELTEK Design

Copyright ©2004-2015 by J. Ronald Adair

All rights reserved. No portion of this book may be reproduced in any form, including electronic media, except by explicit, prior written permission of the publisher. Brief sections may be excerpted for review or comment.

Copyrighted Material

Dedication page

Most of the folks I would dedicate this book to have been dead for many years. Those are the extended family on my mother's side, all with the name of Branstetter (either by birth or marriage). This large family was mostly Oklahoma based and they were the ones that gave me many hours of 42 enjoyment.

Others, more contemporary and too many to mention, read and commented on the book contents, and their suggestions I incorporated and am grateful.

Finally, I dedicate this book to all the old-time 42 players that are still chugging along, keeping the 42 tradition alive.

Table of Contents

INTRODUCTION 9

BACKGROUND OF 42 11

THE BASIC GAME 15
    Preliminaries *15*
    Protocol *17*
    Bidding *18*
    Scoring and Winning *20*
    Direction of Play *21*
    Order of Ranking *23*
    Rules of 42 Domino Play *25*
    Playing a Game *26*

VARIATIONS! 29
    Scoring *30*
    Follow Me *30*
    Small End Lead *31*
    Nello *32*
    Sevens *34*
    Plunge *34*
    Splash *35*

STRATEGY 37
    Bidding *37*
    Offensive Strategy *45*
    Defensive Strategy *51*
    Variations Strategy *55*

ADVANCED STRATEGY 63

TOURNAMENT PLAY 87
    Informal Tournaments *87*
    Formal Tournaments *88*

FORMS FOR YOUR USE 95

MISCELLANEOUS FACTS AND INFORMATION 99

FREQUENTLY ASKED QUESTIONS 101

GLOSSARY 103

BIBLIOGRAPHY 106

INDEX 107

NOTES 110

Table of Figures

Figure 1 The Domino Players – Horace Pippin 10
Figure 2 Map to Garner Texas... 11
Figure 3 Photos of Garner Today 13
Figure 4 Scorecard in play...20
Figure 5 Flow of play 21
Figure 6 Tricks in play 21
Figure 7 Table of Ranks 23
Figure 8 Doubles Option Rankings 33
Figure 9 Bid Setting Table 52
Figure 10 Nello Setting Table 56
Figure 11 Nello Domino Backups 57
Figure 12 Nello Walker Odds Table 58
Figure 13 Sevens Domino Rankings Table 61
Figure 14 Sevens Play Sequence Example 62
Figure 15 Analysis of Plays Table 69
Figure 16 Counters Suit Rankings...71
Figure 17 When to Play Count Table 76
Figure 18 When to Play Offs Table 77
Figure 19 Misdirection Plays Table 78
Figure 20 Plays Analyses Table... 82
Figure 21 Trumps Plays Analyses Table 83
Figure 22 Sample Tournament Program 90
Figure 23 Game Rules Form 95
Figure 24 Score Card Form - Marks 96
Figure 25 Score Card Form – Points.. 97
Figure 26 Bidding Chart 100

[6]

"Killer 42"

'Not Your Daddy's Dominoes'

Forward

The title of this book is 'Killer 42'. What does 'Killer 42' mean? It means the same as in any competitive sport or game, that is, attaining a playing skill that may make a participate a dominating force. This does not mean, however, that all of the techniques covered here will, or should, make you a cutthroat player. That would not be in the spirit of the game, as 42 was originally created for recreation among a group of family and friends. And, that is how the great majority of 42 games are played today. However, nothing is more fun than being in a foursome of very experienced 42 players and watching how the dominos fall by the use of great playing techniques.

So, in the context of the game's 'family and friends' roots, being a killer 42 player means that although we play with a desire to win – even crush the opposition, we do so in a genteel way, with good natured friendliness, manners, and the ultimate goal of everyone having a great time!

Introduction

I was first introduced to the game of "42" at the tender age of eight or so. This happened because the entire extended family on my mother's side were "42" zealots. Every holiday the family gathered at one of our southern Oklahoma homesteads and after lunch, through dinner, and into the late evening hours, multiple card tables would be busy with quartets of moms and dads, aunts and uncles, and grandmother and grandfather. Would this scene make an impression upon an eight- year old? Of course - especially since, like normal kids, we wanted to be a part of all this activity!

But, alas, even though we children were taught the game, we were seldom allowed at the 'grown-ups' tables. This shows how seriously these old folks took their "42" playing!

Back then, I thought "42" was just another game of dominoes, played recreationally by all people in the known universe. Little did I know that it was *not* galactic-wide, but a rather localized phenomenon. And, it was not just a game of dominos, but bordered on a mental disorder!

When I say localized, I mean the game was created just a few miles south of my current home, and, at that time was mostly local to the Texas and Oklahoma areas.

Fortunately, "42" evangelizers over the years have migrated from this area to many points of the compass – taking their zeal of the game with them. Thus today, "42" is being discovered and enjoyed by young and old everywhere.

I started this project years ago at 42 years of age - which I thought was an appropriate age to write a book on '42'. Unfortunately, the demands of earning a living and raising 3 sons shelved the project until just lately. I attribute this restart to two things: finding myself without those financial obligations and with a little more free time, and moving to a new home in the Weatherford, Texas area. The second reason is significant as this small town west of Fort

Worth has an important place in 42 history - and is a 'hot-bed' of '42' practitioners (the next chapter will explain this significance).

So now that it is finished, I hope that if you desire to learn the game of 42, you find that it can help you to not just learn, but even become an accomplished player. If you're already an experienced player, I hope that by explaining the 'whys' of why we play the way we do, this book can make you a 'killer' 42-player!

Disclaimer!

Even though I have been playing 42 for most of my life, I have never played in a formal tournament, have never been world champion nor have the temperament or desire for this level of play. What I do is apply to the game what I have been doing most of my professional life; analyzing and problem solving. I like to explain the 'whys' of how things work, or 'why' we do something a certain way. You might say it is bringing the scientific method to everyday things. So, with that in mind, the goal of this book is to accomplish that very thing with the game of 42.

Figure 1 The Domino Players – Horace Pippin

Background of 42

"The discipline of desire is the background of character."
- John Locke

If you want to plow into the game rules, you can skip this section and go on to the next. However, I sincerely recommend at least a quick glance here as you will learn a little about the history and lore of "42".

The main purpose of this book is to teach readers the game of 42, serve as a comprehensive reference work for experienced 42 players, and heavily focus on strategy and advanced techniques. Hence, I am not spending a great deal of time on the history of the game, and anecdotal accounts of modern players. These areas are covered more comprehensively in several good 42 books such as Dennis Roberson's "Winning 42: Strategy and Lore of the National Game of Texas." However, if you are not knowledgeable, a brief background of how we came to have 42 can help us appreciate the game even more.

If you're a historian, you can look up many published articles by reporters and others such as the article by Christopher Evans published in August 1985 in the Fort Worth Star-Telegram on the history of 42. According to Evans' research, 42 was the creation of two boys in Trappe Spring, Texas in 1887. Trappe Spring, now called Garner, is about 45 miles west of Fort Worth, Texas.

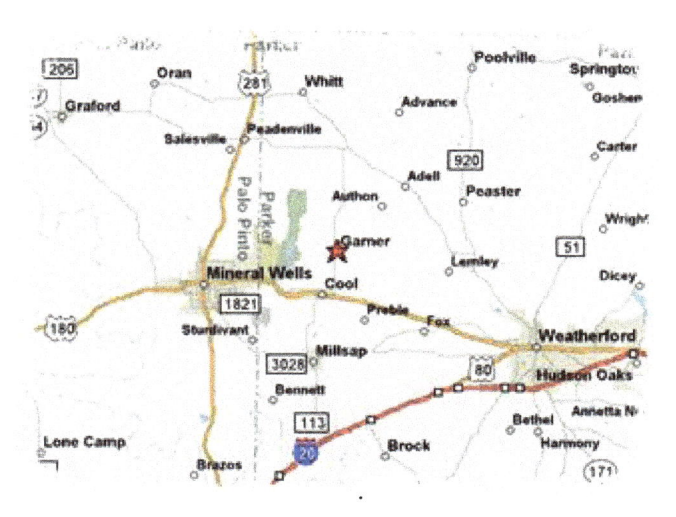

Figure 2 Map to Garner Texas

The story goes that 12-year-old William Thomas and 14-year-old Walter Earl, both avid card players, were punished for playing cards, which many of the local folk thought was sinful. Since *dominos* was an acceptable pastime, the two worked out a domino game resembling the English card game Whist, also known as Pitch. The boys taught the game to their families and the town. When Thomas delivered fruit from his father's orchard to nearby Mineral Wells, Texas, he taught interested bystanders the game. Later, the two families moved to Fannin County in northeast Texas, and 42 apparently took on a life of its own. It was a game that could be played on rural front porches after church services, after Sunday dinner, with "neither shame or sin."

GARNER, TEXAS. Garner is on Farm Road 113 fourteen miles northwest of Weatherford in west central Parker County. The first settlers arrived in the area in the mid-1850s. The twenty or so families who made up the town's population opened a school and called the place Trappe Springs. Development of an established community began in the late 1880s a half mile west of the original site. By 1890 the community had a post office branch and a new name, Garner, chosen in honor of a local gin operator, Ab (or C. B.) Bumgarner. The arrival of the Weatherford, Mineral Wells and Northwestern Railway established Garner as a retail and shipping point for the area. For most of the twentieth century Garner was a church and school community for local farmers. In 1914 it had forty residents and five businesses. The population was seventy-five in 1947 and ninety-eight in 1980 and 1990. The post office was discontinued about 1970.

Some Garner photos follow to give you a flavor for the town:

Entrance to Garner today...   ...the downtown business district (!)

An original country store....and of course there always has to be a school mascot!

Garner is close to midway on the Lake   Trail Way map
Mineral Wells State Trail Way hiking path

And….if you get lost, you can phone home (concrete telephone booth circa 19??)

Figure 3 Photos of Garner Today

Terms and Definitions

"Just definitions either prevent or put an end to a dispute"
- Author Nathaniel Emmons

The following terminology and symbols will be used in the remainder of this book.

- The four players around the table are referred to as Player 1 through Player 4. Players 1 and 3 are partners of one team and Players 2 and 4 are partners of the other team.
- During the bidding phase, the first player to bid will be referred to as Bidder 1 ending with the shuffler as Bidder 4.
- The bid-winner or Declarer will always be referenced as Player 1 and will be the first to start play.
- Trumps will always be red in sample hands.
- A 'trick' and 'round' is synonymous and is a single play of one domino each from each player.
- A 'hand' is the playing of the seven rounds or tricks created from the seven dominos in all of the player's hands and will result in at least a point going to one of the teams.
- A 'game' is defined as the completion of enough 'hands' to total seven points.
- A reference to "T-n" means trump-count – i.e. T-5 means trump suit on one end and a count of 5 on the other.
- All dominoes, whether text or graphics are always shown with the higher end to the left, even though the suit it is part of may be the smaller end.

The Basic Game

"Work and love—these are the basics.
Without them there is neurosis"
*- **Theodor Reik, Psychoanalyst***

While making you a 'killer' 42 player may be the goal, we must first learn the basics. Once we cover these, then we add the variations. Only then, when we move to the Strategies chapter will you begin to learn and apply the playing techniques to move you to the 'killer' level.

Preliminaries

The following sections in this chapter pertain to the basic or standard game of 42. Exceptions and additional rules are covered in the 'Variations' chapter.

42 is played with a standard double six dominos set by four players divided into two teams. Each partner pair faces each other at a four place table.

The game's name comes from the inherent design of the double six domino set upon which the game is based. To illustrate, there are 28 dominos in the set, and there are 5 dominos where the total of the dots (pips) from each side add up to a multiple of 5. These dominos are the five-blank (5), the four-one (5), the three-two (5), the double-five (10), and the six-four (10). If you add up these domino totals (referred to as 'counters'), the total equals 35. The total of the dominos (28) divided by the number of players (4), means that there are 7 rounds in a hand that can be played- ('tricks'). The total of 'counters' (35) plus the seven 'tricks' equals 42 – hence the basis for the name. The object of the game is to collect as many of the 'counters' and 'tricks' to meet or exceed the 'bid' declared by the bid winning team.

Counters:

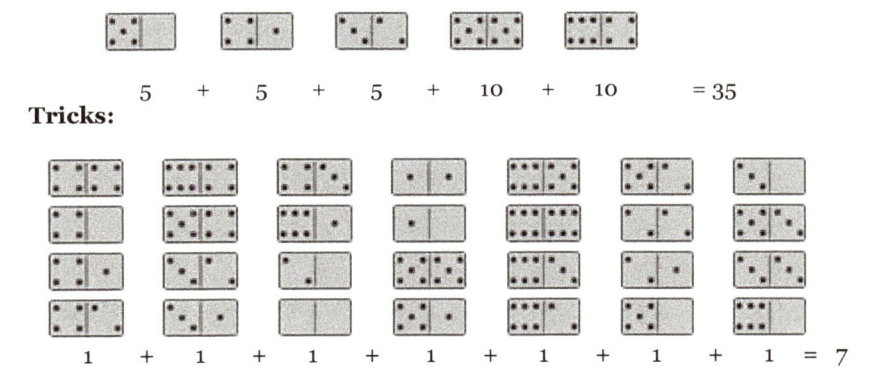

5 + 5 + 5 + 10 + 10 = 35

Tricks:

1 + 1 + 1 + 1 + 1 + 1 + 1 = 7

35 points + 7 tricks = 42!

New Terms Covered:

Team – Two players sitting across from each other at a 4 place table

Pips – Dots on a domino face

Counters – Dominos in a double six set where each end's pips add up to a multiple of 5

Round – A round of one play each from each player – same as a 'trick'. Seven rounds, or tricks make up a hand

Trick - A complete 4 play round equaling a single point (4 dominos)

Bid – The value that a player selects as a goal for his team to reach

Protocol

All games of 42, whether recreational play or tournament, should be governed by a set of basic rules. This is no different than in many other games, but is made somewhat more complex by the many variations in the game that may be chosen. However, the following rules, which are generally acknowledged by the majority of 42 players, should apply:

- **Reneging**
  If a domino is played, then that play should stand unless you have not properly followed the lead. You may replace the domino as long as it is your turn, but if the following player has played his turn and it is discovered that you did not follow lead, then it is a 'renege' and your team forfeits that hand. There is no penalty if you switch out so as to properly follow lead, but your team has created a disadvantage because of showing one of your un-played dominos. It is not allowable to change out your played domino to play a better one during your turn.
- **Communication**
  Outside of friendly conversation, do not talk across the table. Most tournaments require no talking across the table during the play of each hand. Talking is allowed after all have played their dominoes.
- **Misplaying**
  Playing out of turn is a misplay. For recreational play, you have only created a disadvantage for your team. For tournament play, it is a loss of turn.
- **'Lay down' Hand**
  If the hand is over, "lay it down." How do you know it is over? If you've already met your bid or you're guaranteed to win the rest of the dominoes. Actually, you lay 'down' your hand by placing your dominoes face-up so that everyone can see them, just to prove you will win it no matter what. As an example, if all the trumps have been played and you have nothing but doubles or 'walkers' and are in the lead, there is no possible way you can lose. Or, if you only need one more point to make your bid and you have the highest remaining trump, just show that trump to prove you will make your bid. Laying down your hand in these situations helps the game to move on without wasting time.
- **Handling of the dominoes**
  The dominos should be shuffled by the player whose turn it is to shuffle and all players will pull 7 dominos each with the dealer receiving the remaining 7. If a player mistakenly selects more than 7 and has 'set' them where he can see them, then the shorted player may choose any of the dominos in the player's hand with the excess for his 7th domino. In tournament play this may mean a forfeiture of the hand. If it is a hand with a bid of a 'mark' or more, stack the dominoes two tricks upon each other so that only the last two tricks are showing. This is usually optional for recreational play. For bids under a mark, always let everyone see what dominoes you've already won.

- **Bidding**
  Do not bid out of turn and don't pass before it is your turn to bid. You cannot change your bid after you have made it. A bid of 'X over (a particular player)' that has not bid is not allowed. Remember, bid on your turn only.
- **'Signaling'**
  Signaling or tipping your partner to what you may have, what you may need, or when to play a certain way during recreational play is considered bad manners and goes against the spirit of playing for the enjoyment of the game and association with good company. For tournament play, signaling will mean forfeiture of the game and an invitation to seek company elsewhere. Signaling is usually done by domino pointing, hand or body signals or verbal cues. However, legitimate signals that are allowed in recreational and tournament play are generally understood bidding and playing patterns. Remember, 42 is a great way for four or more people to enjoy friendly association and recreation.

Bidding

The game of 42 is based upon a bid and match method. The team with the highest bid starts the play, and must meet or exceed their bid. Bidding is started by the winning draw (from above), and goes around the table to all four players. The highest bid determines the starting player. The minimum bid is 30 and the maximum is 42 points, or one 'mark' (more than one mark can be bid with different variations – for now we will define just the basic game). A maximum of two marks can be bid in basic 42 unless it has already been bid and three marks are required for a higher bid (see Bidding Chart, page 99). Since play is based upon two teams, the bid is the *team's* bid even though either member of the team makes a bid. Obviously the second member of the team would not overbid his partner unless there was, in his mind, a good reason to do so. An example of this would be if Bidder 1 opened bidding at 30, the next player bids 31 or higher, and Bidder 2 has a good enough hand to have a chance to garner more points than the previous opponents' bid. This prevents the opposing team winning the bid (more on these steps are covered in the chapter on strategy).

If the bidding team makes their bid, then they win the hand. If they do not make their bid, then they go 'set', and the opposing team wins the hand.

New Terms Covered:

Renege – failing to play at the right time or the right required domino

Lay down hand – a hand you may have that is unbeatable

Shuffle - Mixing up the full set of 28 dominos to prepare them for play

Signaling – A practice by low life types of secretly transmitting information to their partners so as to gain an unfair advantage

Pointing – A type of signaling by using the domino itself to point to another to indicate to his partner what the player may have (bad!)

Mark – All of the available points in a hand, i.e. 42

Hand - Seven passes (rounds) around the table (7 'tricks' or all 28 dominos played)

Set – The result of a team not making their bid

Stacked Tricks – When a 1 or more mark bid is declared, tricks are stacked 2 upon 2 so that only the last 2 tricks are visible

Scoring and Winning

The standard way of scoring is that the winning team receives a point for each hand won (bid made). The game ends with the first team gaining a total of seven points. The accepted way of tracking the points won is adding each stroke to the letters making up the word 'ALL' (go ahead, count 'em, there are seven strokes). This applies to 'mark' only scoring – for 'points' scoring, see the Variations chapter.

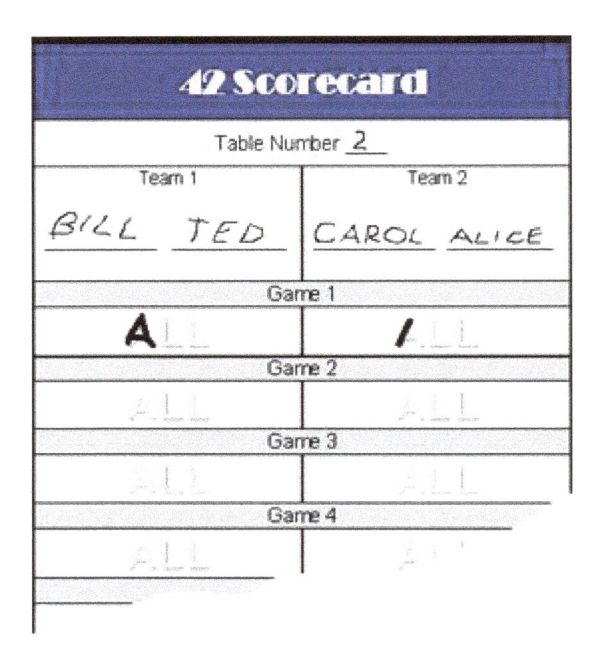

Figure 4 Scorecard in play

Direction of Play

The player with the winning bid begins play and the play continues in a clockwise direction (as seen from above), ending with player four for that hand.

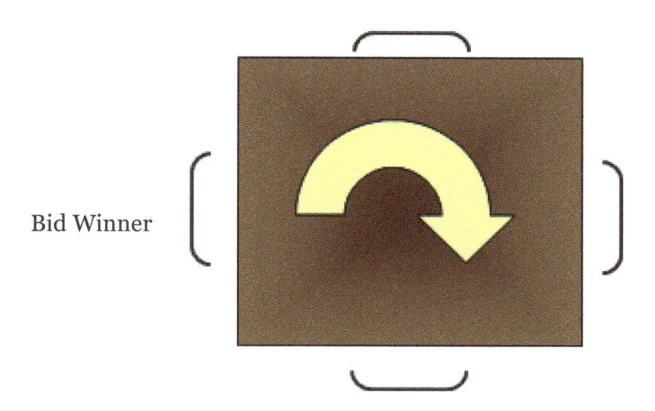

Bid Winner

Figure 5 Flow of play

Each four-domino 'trick' is moved face-up to the winning bidder's partner's right-hand position, with each successive trick joined to it as follows:

Bid-Winner

Figure 6 Tricks in play

If the bid is 1 mark or more, then only the last two tricks are shown, so they are stacked two upon two.

[21]

Trumps and Leads

42 is based, like numerous card games, upon trumps and leads. A trump suit is declared by the winning bidder before play commences. A lead is a non-trump suit with which a player leads a hand. As is common with other games, leads must be followed unless a player is void in that lead. If this happens, then there are 2 choices that can be exercised – either to play a trump or discard an 'off' domino (a domino that is neither trump or a lead).

If a trump is led, then all players must play a trump if they have it, else they may play a counter (if they are the partner to the leading player), or a non-value 'off' if they are the opposing team. A Trump may be declared even if the winning bidder is void in that suit (although not a likely practice); a trump does not have to be led after declaration, but another suit may be led instead (more common). See the strategy chapter for more on these points. Trumps may be any suit between 0 (blanks) and six, and may also be doubles. In addition, there are several variations where there is no trump declared.

Trump examples (trumps shown in red in all following examples):

Five trump:

Doubles trump:

New Terms covered:
Suit - Seven dominos with one side having the same number of pips
Trump – A declared suit by the winning bidder
Lead – A suit determined by the first non-trump domino played by a player in a round
Off - A domino that is worthless in the current lead round

Order of Ranking

One of the most confusing aspects of 42 is how the dominos are ranked per side and which side applies at what time. Mental lapses of beginning (and some experienced) players usually are caused by this very thing. The rule is that if a domino is led, it is understood that the lead is the *high end* of the domino. The exception is the small end lead explained in the Variations chapter. All dominos following the first lead played will have the one side with that lead suit, and the other side will be from a six (highest) to a blank (lowest). An exception to this is trumps: the trump is *always* the lead no matter how many pips are on the opposite end. To help understand how this plays out consider the following chart (ranking from highest order to lowest):

6 Lead	5 Lead	4 Lead	3 Lead	2 Lead	1 Lead	0 Lead	Dbls Lead*
6-6	5-5	4-4	3-3	2-2	1-1	0-0	6-6
6-5	5-6	4-6	3-6	2-6	1-6	0-6	5-5
6-4	5-4	4-5	3-5	2-5	1-5	0-5	4-4
6-3	5-3	4-3	3-4	2-4	1-4	0-4	3-3
6-2	5-2	4-2	3-2	2-3	1-3	0-3	2-2
6-1	5-1	4-1	3-1	2-1	1-2	0-2	1-1
6-0	5-0	4-0	3-0	2-0	1-0	0-1	0-0

* There is no 'Doubles suit' lead except in Doubles as trump or 'Follow-Me' (No-trump)

Figure 7 Table of Ranks

We can see that the dominos in the blue squares when played as leads, have the left side defining the lead suit. The dominos in the yellow squares are NEVER leads from the perspective of the left side – they will be considered that suit ONLY as a following play from a blue square lead. As an example, all of the left side 6's set the lead suit as a 6. All of the 5's do EXCEPT the 5-6 – if it is led, it is considered a 6. All of the 4's except the 4-6 and 4-5 are 4 leads – the 4-6 is considered a 6 suit lead, and the 4-5 is considered a 5 suit lead. As you can see, the only 0 left side that can be played as a suit lead is the 0-0 – the other 0's are 6,5,4,3,2 or 1 suit leads.

It becomes evident that the lower the point count on both ends becomes (except for the double), the value of that domino becomes less as a lead. For example, any 0 suit led other than the double would not catch any 0 domino as the opposite end would set the lead suit.

If the Small End Lead variation is declared and the player names the small end as lead, for example the 1-6, then the suit is 1 and the only domino catching the 1-6 would be the double 1 (1-1).

Now we can see why beginner mistakes are made here! But, there's more.

Trumps are different than non-trump leads as the end with the trump suit always declares the lead and the opposite end determines the value or ranking of the lead.

Trumps are a suit unto themselves. They are NOT a part of a lead suit based upon the opposite end value from the trump suit end.

To summarize:

>1) Whether a domino is a trump lead or a non-trump lead determines which side is the lead suit and which side is the ranking value.
>2) If you follow a lead by another player and your domino has a higher number of pips on the non-lead side than any others played, then your domino 'catches' the trick.
>3) All of the remaining suits after the trump has been declared consist of six dominos only – the missing domino being a part of the 'trump' suit.

Consider this 'Majestic Error' Example:

You have in your hand the following dominos –

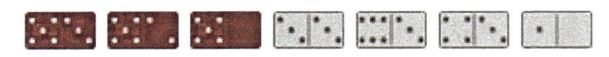

Fives have been declared trump, which you have 3. You have gained the lead with your second trump play and on the next round you lead out the double 3. However, a mental lapse has overtaken you and you see that you also have two of the next highest threes, the 3-6 and the 3-4.
So, after taking the double 3 trick, you follow with the next highest 3, the 3-6. Alas, your opponent to your left promptly plays his double 6 (the real suit), your partner reluctantly plays his 6-1 (instead of the trump in his hand), and your opponent to your right promptly sets you by tossing in his 6-4. If trumps had been threes however, this would have been the proper play and you would still be in the lead (and not set).

By all means, learn and practice these relationships – it will help prevent you from making a bone-head play later (yes, it can happen!).

Rules of 42 Domino Play

There are three simple rules governing what *type* domino must be played:

Rule #1: A player **must** follow the lead played if he has a domino of that suit that is **not** a trump.

Rule #2: Trumps are a **suit** of their own – a domino that has one end with the lead and the other with a trump does **not** have to be played as a lead follow-on.

Rule #3: If a player is void in the lead, he **may** play a trump, a counter, or an off, depending upon the circumstances.

Playing a Game

We assume that who will be partners has been determined by mutual agreement or by drawing dominos. When drawing, the dominos are shuffled and each player draws a domino. The player who draws the highest domino (total pip count), will be the scorekeeper, and the next highest domino holder will be his partner. The two lowest domino holders will be the opposing team partners. In case of tie(s), those players each draw another domino to break the tie.

To initially start the game, the scorekeeper shuffles ('shakes') the dominos face-down. To determine who starts the first game shuffle, each player draws a domino. The player drawing a domino with the highest pip count (both ends summed) is the starting shuffler. After this player shuffles, all players select seven dominos each with the shuffler choosing last. The dominos each player select are placed on edge facing them, where the faces cannot be seen by the other players. Some players hold the dominoes in their hands, but you might find this a little awkward. A commonly used arrangement (and usually a tournament requirement), is to place your seven dominos on edge in two rows of 4 and 3 dominos facing you. The player to the left of the shuffler starts the bidding. The next hand shuffle then moves to the next player in a clockwise direction.

When the winning bid is determined, the winning bidder declares the trump suit, if applicable, and he may also declare a variation. He then begins play by playing his first domino. Each successive player must then follow suit or play per the rules as previously defined. The trick, if taken by the bidding team is moved to the Declarer's partner's right hand position by the Declarer's partner. If the trick is taken by the defensive team, the trick is moved to the right hand position of the number four player (the second defensive team member). Each four domino trick is positioned four side by side as shown earlier. When the hand is complete, the points for each team are counted from these respective collections of tricks. If the bidding teams bid total is met before the completion of the seven tricks, then the hand can be declared won and play can end. Or, if the bidding team has nothing but trumps and-or doubles as his remaining dominos and all other trumps are in, then the play can end at that point. The player holding this hand can declare he has the rest and lays his dominos face-up.

If the defensive team takes a trick started by the bidding team, then that player playing the high lead domino starts play for the next round by playing a lead of his choosing. Depending upon which player takes the trick with the highest domino, the lead switches from the offensive team to the defensive team and back until all seven tricks are played, or enough count is in for the bidding team's bid count or they go set.

If the bidding team makes its bid, then a 'mark' is made on the score pad to start the first letter of the word 'ALL'. If the defensive team 'sets' the bidding team, then they add the mark under their names on the score pad.

This, in essence, is the basic 42 hand.

To summarize from all of the previous points:

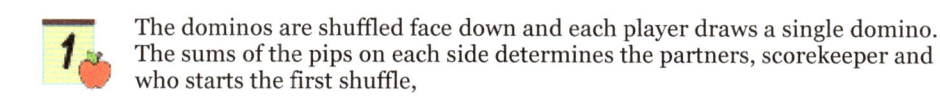

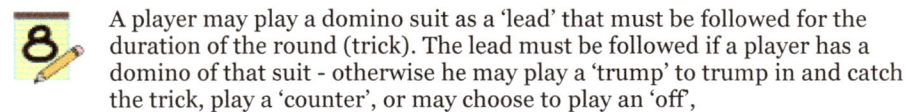

1. The dominos are shuffled face down and each player draws a single domino. The sums of the pips on each side determines the partners, scorekeeper and who starts the first shuffle,

2. The dominos are shuffled by the player determined from above step – each player draws 7 dominos, the shuffler drawing last,

3. The player to the shuffler's left starts the bidding, bidding progresses around the table ending with the shuffler,

4. The bid must start at 30 and can be as high as 42 (a 'mark'), or 84 (2 marks), unless one or two marks are already bid and then the bid can be a mark higher than the previous high bid,

5. The winning bidder or Declarer (Player 1) starts play, his partner (Player 3) of his team, (offense) sits across from him, the defensive team are the remaining two players (Players 2 and 4),

6. The Declarer names a domino suit as the trump (unless it is a no-trump hand). The trump suit remains trumps for the duration of the hand,

7. The winning bidder's team attempts to collect as many counters and tricks as possible so as to make their bid,

8. A player may play a domino suit as a 'lead' that must be followed for the duration of the round (trick). The lead must be followed if a player has a domino of that suit - otherwise he may play a 'trump' to trump in and catch the trick, play a 'counter', or may choose to play an 'off',

9. The team that 'takes' the trick moves the 4 dominos to the right hand position of the respective team's partner,

10. When all seven tricks have been played, the count is tabulated – if the bidding team makes their bid or above, they get a mark, if not, the defensive team gets a mark,

11. When enough hands are played so that one team gets 7 marks, then the game is over.

CONCLUSION

That is the basics of the game in a nutshell. It would be helpful for beginning players to play a few games of this basic 42 so as to get the hang of it. Once you feel comfortable at this level, move on to the next chapter, **'Variations'** to add the fun stuff.

Variations!

"Nature is an endless combination and repetition of a very few laws. She hums the old well-known air through innumerable variations"
*- **Ralph Waldo Emerson***

Now that we've got the Basic 42 game under our belt, it is time to learn some fun variations and additions. These will add a lot of richness to the game and more fully utilize the domino combinations that will be dealt. It is important that the variations that are not a part of the standard game and would like to be played be agreed upon by the players *before* the game begins. To assist players to determine what variations to allow, it will be helpful to define the 'standard' 42 rules. Not everyone may agree with this definition as different options may be included or not depending upon the family or local traditions. However, the following definition is based upon a consensus of many experienced players, organizations and other reference works:

'Basic 42'

Variations can be of two types – options to the Basic 42 game and completely different styles of play referred to as 'contracts'. First, let's cover the several options for the Basic 42 game. These are:

- Bidding — Forced
- Scoring — By Marks
- Follow Me — Allowed
- Small End Lead — Allowed (first trick only)
- Nello — Not allowed
- Sevens — Not allowed
- Plunge — Not allowed
- Splash — Not allowed

Variations can be of two types – options to the Basic 42 game and completely different styles of play referred to as 'contracts'. First, let's cover the several options for the Basic 42 game. These are:

- Bidding
- Scoring
- Follow Me
- Small End Lead

Bidding

There are two ways to handle the bidding phase. One is to re-shuffle and re-draw if there are no bids from any player, i.e. each player passes on their turn. The other, more accepted option is to make the fourth bid 'forced'. This means that if Bidder 1 through 3 passes, Bidder 4 must open play with a bid of 30. Most players like this option as it can add a little recklessness to the game. If the Nello contract is allowed with the 'dropped bid' variation, then the bidding must be 'forced'.

Scoring

Even though the original scoring method of the game was by points (from the Whist and Pitch roots), the scoring choice most recognized and used today is to score by 'marks' as explained in the previous chapter. However, some players like to play by points. Scoring by points adds some nuance to the strategy during play, but on the down-side takes more time for the game. If the players elect to score by points, then the following rules apply:

- The bids are the numbers from 30 to 42, then 84 and 168. You cannot bid 168 unless someone has bid 84.
- For bids below 42, if Declarer's team makes their bid, both sides score the points they take. If the Declarer's team goes set, they score zero, and the opponents score the points they take plus Declarer team's bid.
- For bids of 42, 84 and 168, Declarer's team scores the bid if successful. If Declarer is set the opponents gain the Declarer's team bid but nothing for their tricks.

Follow Me

Follow Me, otherwise known as 'no trumps' is an interesting variation that is part of the Basic 42 definition. The rules of play are as usual, except that there are no trumps and a trick is always won by the highest domino of the suit led.

To play, the bid-winner declares 'follow me', just like he would declare trump. In effect he is saying 'no trumps'.
Although not naming a trump suit, he does have the choice between how the doubles are treated. These choices are:

- **Doubles high** - the double is the highest domino of each suit (as normal)
- **Doubles low** - the double is lowest in each suit (for example the double 6 is beaten by all dominoes of the six suit, even the 6-0)

Some players only allow the bidder to choose Follow Me when playing for all the tricks - that is, bidding 42 (one mark) or higher. The most common is to allow bids from 30 up, just like in Basic 42.
How does Follow Me work?
To declare Follow Me, the bid-winner would have a hand that has only one, two or three high dominos across several suits. All rules pertaining to leads apply, there are just no trumps.

A sample 'Follow Me' hand:

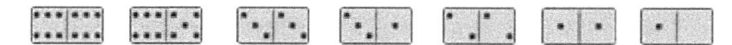

In this hand, we would play the 6-6 and 6-5 and see if the 6-4 comes in on these two tricks. If it did not, then we would have the choice to continue with the 3-3, 2-2, and 1-1, or the 1-0 off in the hopes your partner may catch it for a round (to throw off the 3-1). If the defensive team catches the 1-0, then you have 2 high dominos to try to catch their next lead. What would set you is if the defensive team caught your 1-0 and led back with the 6-4 and 5-5.

It takes a trained eye to recognize a Follow Me hand while being in the habit of looking for a normal 42 trump-based hand. Study some sample Follow Me hands so as to make it as automatic as possible.

Small End Lead

The accepted *Small End Lead* variation is for only the first lead of the hand and is in lieu of leading a trump on the first play. The advantage of this is that it can allow a player to discard an 'off' domino at the time when it is better played. From the previous chapter, the rule is that all leads default to the larger end that sets the lead value. So, a small end lead is the opposite of this and consequently has to be stated by the player when the first domino is laid down (again, this does not pertain to trumps). Since a small end lead is always lower than the double, the double of that suit will catch it. For instance, if a 6-1 is lead as a small end lead (1-6), then a 1-1 (double 1), will be the highest of the suit and will catch the trick. That is, in essence, the purpose of this type lead – that is to force the opposing team to catch the trick at the beginning of the game with a valuable domino (a double), and clean an undesirable one from the bidder's hand.

Sample hand where a small end lead could be appropriate:

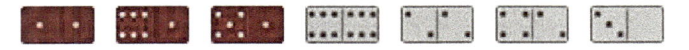

We see that trumps are the 1 suit. The bidder has won the bid at a high bid and cannot lose a 10 counter. He also has 2 offs, the 4-2 and the 3-0. The more dangerous of the two is the 4-2 since when it is led, it can draw out the 6-4, a 10 counter. Knowing this the Declarer names 1's as trump and starts the round with the 4-2 but names it as a small end lead, i.e. the 2. This means that 2 is the suit and the count is 4. The dominos that can catch this lead are the 2-2, 6-2, and 5-2 and there is a counter in that suit, the 3-2. This lead accomplishes dumping an undesirable domino that could be a problem later. There is also a 33% chance that his partner has the 2-2 and in addition, a chance that one of the defensive players will not throw the 3-2 if they do not know if their partner has the 2-2 or not.

Proper use of the Small End Lead can create a winning hand by eliminating *randomness* that may make it a losing one.

Now, we'll explain variations that are not a part of Basic 42. These are the 'contracts'. They are:

- Nello (Low Boy, Low)
- Sevens
- Plunge
- Splash

Nello

Nel-O or Nello, to my knowledge, is the oldest contract variation. As such, for recreational play I would include it as a part of Basic 42 as long as it can be called only by the last bidder with the opening bid 'dropped' on him (i.e. the first three players pass). However, because one player has to refrain from the hand in Nello, it is usually not allowed in formal tournament play. Some players in recreational play allow any winning bidder to call a Nello contract, but be forewarned that many players are Nello fanatics and may call Nello at the drop of a hat. This results in their partner not getting to play much, so I would not recommend this option. However, a compromise variation is allowing the shuffler to call a Nello even if the bid is 30 or above - that is, it is not forced (dropped) upon him. This is a nice compromise as it allows Nello to be played a little more, but not to the point of distraction.

Nello, is a fun variation as it messes with the mind. Why? Because, where in Basic 42 the team strives for the *maximum* points gained, in Nello, the object is collecting the *minimum* possible, i.e. zero points.

Just imagine - the game has been progressing with all players thinking "get most points, get most points" and a Nello contract is called. The mental process instantly must switch to "get no points, get no points!" The following gives a quick view of Nello rules:

- Bidding – Minimum bid is one mark (42) automatically since no tricks may be captured by the bidder. However, 2 marks may be bid if desired (or more to gain bid if one or more marks have already been bid).
- Who plays? – The Nello bidder plays against the opposing team. His partner does not play and must lay his dominos face down for the duration of the hand.
- Goal of the hand – The object of the Nello contract is for the bidder to avoid capturing a single trick. This means after his opening lead, the opposing team players must be in the lead and capture all seven tricks between them.
- Trumps – there are no trumps in Nello. It is played like Follow Me (except YOU want to follow, not lead).
- Counters – counters are irrelevant in Nello since it is an all or nothing bid model - one lost trick will set you and gives one or more marks to the other team.

Traditionally, you are able to change the rank of doubles in a suit whenever you call Nello. You can leave doubles normal ('doubles take the trick' or 'doubles high'), make them the lowest domino in the suit ('doubles low'), or make them not in the suit at all ('doubles catch doubles'). Not everyone plays with each of these options. Make sure to determine this before you start the game. However, playing with all of them adds a lot of fun to the game.

The following table shows the domino rankings with each of these doubles declarations (6 suit is used as example):

Doubles Call	Domino Rank
'Doubles High'	(dominoes ranked high to low)
'Doubles Low'	(dominoes ranked high to low)
'Doubles take Doubles' (Doubles are ranked 6-6 highest to 0-0 lowest)	(dominoes ranked high to low)

Figure 8 Doubles Option Rankings

A successful Nello hand is a combination of the right dominos in the Declarer's hand, the right dominos falling from the defensive team players, and some good strategy by the Nello bidder. We will cover this Nello strategy in the **Strategy** chapter.

The following contracts are not as commonly played as Nello, but if you are played out with 42 and its variations up to this point, and have gotten bored (!), then these are some fun variations for recreational play.

Sevens

If the rules have been agreed beforehand, players may bid on 'Sevens'. When you call Sevens, forget all the rules of normal 42. Sevens, like Nello, are always bid in marks starting with one or two. This means that the bid-winner must catch every trick. When the player winning the bid calls 'sevens', then each domino played must equal 7 as the sum of the pips on both ends of the domino. If it does not equal 7, the closest to 7 wins the trick. If two or more players play dominoes that are equal in pips, the first one played wins the trick and gets to lead the next one. Note that the total itself doesn't matter - only how close it is to 7. So, a 6 and an 8 count the same since they are both 'one away.' The lead can switch from the bid-winner and to his partner and back again, and as long as this happens, the hand will be won for that team.

A good Sevens hand would have at least two 7 totals, 2 or more 6 or 8 totals, and 2 or more 5 or 9 totals. It should not have the 6-6 or 0-0 unless you want to gamble on your partner catching the trick that you lead with either of these dominos.

There is not much of a defensive strategy against a Sevens call as one must play the domino with the nearest total pips to 7 and hope that you OR your partner has a nearer to seven total than both players of the bid-winning team. The first domino played of a specific total is the one that counts. Obviously, once the Declarer starts play, if several players count totals equals his, he catches the trick since he has played first. Because of this, the bid-winner has an advantage during play (as long as he stays in the lead).

Playing a domino other than the nearest is not allowed and is reneging. However, remember all it takes is for your team to catch just one trick to set your opponents.

Plunge

When you call plunge, you must have **four** doubles in your hand. Without you saying anything about what you have, your partner picks trumps. You, the declarer, leads the first domino. If you plunge, you have to bid four marks (or higher if that's already been reached). This is the only exception to the two mark opening limit on bids. Note: some people will limit plunge (and splash - see below) to two marks instead of four so as to keep the normal two mark limit.

Splash

This is the same as plunge, except it only requires **three** doubles in your hand and only a three mark bid. Many people will play plunge but not splash, so be certain this is determined at the start of the game.

CONCLUSION

The previous two sections will teach you how to play basic 42 and how to add to your basic 42 knowledge all of the accepted variations. At this point, your chances of winning your 42 game is based upon a **100% randomness** of the dominos dealt and how they fall during the hand. However, to graduate from this random level play to 'killer' level play, we want to decrease that randomness factor and put more control into how we play our hand. This reduces the **random factor** from 100% to a minor part of the equation. How do we do this? We do it by applying strategic decisions to our plays. We can learn how in the following sections on **Strategy**.

New Terms covered:

Variation – An option to the Basic 42 model, or a different way of playing

Contract – A non-standard variation of 42 such as Nello

Strategy

"The most dangerous strategy is to jump a chasm in two leaps"
- Benjamin Disraeli

As in sports or war, strategy in 42 can mean the difference between winning and losing. However, you will find that during the course of a game, the pace will be too fast for a comprehensive analysis using the points in this chapter (and, would be considered discourteous). That is why you should study them so as to understand how they work, and learn to recognize patterns that point to certain strategic plays. This way you can react quickly as play progresses.

Strategy in 42 covers three areas; **1**) analyzing your hand and making the appropriate bid, **2**) offensive strategy, and **3**) defensive strategy. We will cover these three areas of the game plus the variations strategy in this chapter. We will then conclude this chapter with *Advanced Strategy*.

Bidding

The first strategy in bidding is to do what you can to **gain the bid**. The reason for this is that bidders statistically have the advantage in winning the hand as they are in control and can make choices. The defenders must always react. *A strong trump hand in your opponent's possession becomes useless if he does not get the bid to play it!* However, bidding intelligently is the key, as reckless bidding will skew the advantage to the defensive team. Hence, the bidding strategies in this section are the first steps to winning the hand.

Before we inspect positional bidding strategies, it is helpful to define the four types of hands a player may have in his possession. These hand definitions are very critical to understanding biding strategy, so be sure to realistically assess your drawn hand. They are:

- 'Junk' hand – a hand with few high dominos, few consecutives of a suit, no counters, etc.
- 'Helper' hand – a hand with inadequate dominos that can make a playable trump suit, but can have a number of counters, and one or two doubles.
- 'Average Trump' hand – a hand with a minimum of 3 dominos including the double and next highest of a trump suit, one or two doubles and a counter or two.
- 'Strong Trump' hand – a hand with at least the top 3 high in the trump suit, and at least 2 doubles including the double 6 and-or double 5, and no more than 1 or 2 'offs' - those offs only able to draw a 5 counter.

Bidding strategy is very dependent upon your playing position in the hand. That is, bid position strategy varies from the first through the fourth bidder. The following analysis is from the perspective of each of these four bidding positions (Basic 42 only):

First or Opening Position –

- The opening bid position has the only opportunity to *always* be able to bid 30. First, you must realize that your hand plus your partners plus the odds of how the dominos fall, makes it very possible that you can make a 30 bid (you can loose 2 tricks with 5 pointers each or 2 tricks – one with a 10 pointer and still make 30). However, a bid of 31 reduces the odds somewhat. The opening bidder is in position to affect all subsequent positions' bidding strategy, even his partner's.

Now, let's analyze this position from the perspective of the four hands defined above.

If you have a....

Junk Hand
Action:
> Pass and hope your partner can carry the mail (unless Nello is allowed for any player, then look closely!).

Helper Hand
Action:
> You should probably pass as you can go set with free counters in your hand and no trumps. If your partner has a biddable hand, then you are in a good position to help him. If one of your opponents gets the bid, you may have an opportunity to set him.

Note: It is important, if you are in bidding position one, to not open a bid of 30 on a marginal hand such as the two previous ones. The reason for this is that your bid of 30 raises the minimum bid to 31 that your partner has to bid (assuming the opponents are passing). He may have a slightly better hand than you, i.e. a 30 bid hand that could be attainable, but not a 31 hand. There should be a tacit understanding between the two of you that the partner occupying Bidder 3 should be the one to bid on marginal hands if required.

Average Trump Hand
Action:
> You should bid 31 or higher with consideration of what you can loose and still make bid. This action signals your partner that you have a playable hand. Unless he has a very strong hand he will normally let you have it unless he is afraid to let Bidder 4 overbid you. If Bidder 2 overbids you, then Bidder 3 should bid his hand and take his chances with Bidder 4.

Strong Trump Hand
Action:
> With a very strong hand like this you should bid at least 36. This makes any following bidder with a higher bid eligible to go set by losing a 5 count trick. Many players bid a mark on a strong hand. Either bid signals your partner that he should let you run with the hand.

Second Position –

The second bid position has to respond to what the opening bidder does. If that player passes, then in essence, Bidder 2 becomes Bidder 1 and the above choices can generally apply. The only exception is now there is only one opposing player to contend with. This throws the team advantage to your team 2-1 (from above, Bidder 1 will have a junk or helper hand). In this case, you should consider an opening bid of 30 even on a hand that is not as strong as you would like, thus forcing player 3 to bid 31 if he wants the bid, and if he does, you have your partner as a last chance to obtain bid.

Third Position –

The third position (partner to opening bidder), is unique with a lot of choices to respond to. The following are some scenarios that will be faced by Bidder 3:

> *Condition*
> **Action:**
> Partner (Bidder 1) opens with a 30 bid and Bidder 2 passes.
>
> From above, Bidder 3 knows that his partner has an average hand and also knows that Bidder 2 has a junk-helper-setting hand. If your hand is above average, then you might want to up the bid to 31 so as to force Bidder 4 to bid at least 32 to get the bid.
>
> *Condition*
> Bidder 1 passes, Bidder 2 opens with a 30 bid.
> **Action:**
> This scenario tells you your partner has either a junk or helper hand. If you have a strong trump hand, but are fairly void in counters, then the odds may indicate he has a helper hand. Of course, Bidder 2 or 4 may have a lot of counters, but if Bidder 2 did he would probably bid higher than 30 so as to gain the bid. That leaves Bidder 4 who may have a lot of counters. If he does, then he would probably not have a strong trump hand to up both Bidder 2's bid and yours. In this case, you should bid 31 or higher if your hand supports it. If Bidder 4 bids above this, then your partner has the count and Bidder 4 has a very strong hand and has a good chance to make his bid.
>
> *Condition*
> Bidders 1 and 2 pass.
> **Action:**
> There are several possibilities with this condition – both players have junk hands, or one has a junk hand and the other a helper hand. Both could have helper hands but the count may not be enough to go around, especially if you have a counter. Since this masks what your partner may have, you may be on your own, so bid accordingly. Remember though that you do not want Bidder 4 to get the bid cheap, so if your hand supports it, make the bid higher than 30.
>
> *Condition*
> Bidder 1 opens with a higher bid (31 or higher).
> **Action:**
> If you have a helper hand, then do not bid. If Bidder 2 ups your partner's bid, then you may opt to up his bid, but the chance that Bidder 4 may have a setting hand still exists. However, there may not be much to loose as Bidder 2 apparently has a fairly strong hand to up the strong opening bid. In summary, you should up it and play so as to hope your partner can gain the lead for a few rounds (he probably has a few doubles to play).

Fourth or Final Position –

The fourth bid position is in some sense, the easiest, and outside of the opening position, the most powerful. For one thing, if you are allowing Nello, Bidder 4 has this variation as another option to play in the case of getting stuck with a 'junk' hand. If you are Bidder 4 and everyone passes and you also have a poor hand, then you learn from this that most of the suits and doubles are fairly well distributed among all four players. In this case, if the hand is not bad enough for a Nello bid, then you will probably have enough of a hand to start a 30 bid, with the chance of your partner gaining the lead and between the two of you eking out your bid. Take heart if this happens as often when a bid is forced on Bidder 4, the bid is made. If any of the Bidder 1-3 scenarios listed previously take place, then you have the option of viewing the entire playing strategy before having to make your own. Good analysis from these positional strategies, can give an experienced player a good feel for where counters may be, who has trump suits (and as play progresses, what those trumps would have been), and who have the 'junk' hands (see following **Advanced Strategies** for more on this).

Bidding Strategy if Scoring is by Points

If you are scoring by points the bidding strategies to this point are valid. However, there is a bidding effect that can result if scoring is by points.

That is, since by the nature of the points scoring rules, the team with the weaker hand may tend to bid less or not at all and wait until a better hand. This is because they can still gain points on their weak hand if the offensive team makes their bid and can lose many points if they bid and go set. This applies also to the team with the stronger hand – they will tend to bid lower since going set gives the opposing team an even larger bonanza. The net result is a more conservative approach with less 'roll the dice' playing.

There is one subtle bidding strategy. If Bidder 4 inherits a forced 30 bid, he could bid Nello instead of chancing going set on a 30 bid. How does this work? Since the opponents get the bidding teams bid PLUS whatever points they catch, if you go set on a 30 bid your opponents would receive 43 points or more (30 + at least 13 points - minimum required to set). If you go set on a failed Nello attempt, it would restrict the opponents to a maximum of 42 points.

Opening Hand Analysis

The following is analysis of some randomly drawn hands to illustrate bidding strategy.

Basic 42

'Junk Hand'

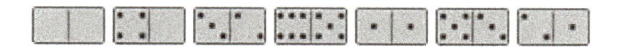

This hand has something for everyone – a few 'almost' trump suits, a small counter, a couple of doubles, and some fairly bad offs. In essence, it is a typical 'junk' hand and should not be bid on. However, if it is the case that the bid is forced upon you, then there are three choices for trumps, the 0 suit, the 1 suit, and the 5 suit. If you choose the 0 or 1 suit for trumps, then you are left with only one double lead. If you choose 5's for trump, then you would have two double leads. But you have a good chance to draw (and lose) 10 or 15 points with either 5 lead. If 0 is trump, then a 5 counter, the 5-0 can catch the 4-0. The same with the 1 suit as the 4-1 would catch the 2-1. The trump choice should be either the 0 or 1 with only a 5 counter at jeopardy and the 10 counters at risk only via randomness and your partner's hand. More than 31 should not be bid on this hand as it is likely you will lose at least a 10 counter.

'Helper hand'

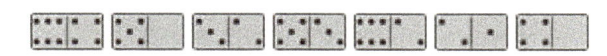

This hand does not have enough of the right dominos to string together to make a trump suit, but it does have 20 points in counters. These are terrible offs but they also make you the player to make or break bids. It is also not bad enough to qualify as a Nello hand, if it was eligible, so don't try it. Let this one go and be a helper to your partner if he gets the bid, or lie in wait with count if your partner catches one of your opponent's tricks.

'Average Trump Hand'

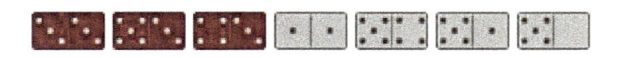

This is an example of one of many average trump hands. The best trump suit would be the 3's as shown. There is one double lead, the 1-1. However the offs are of a dangerous suit, the 5. There is the chance, though, that the 5-5 could be played on one of your trump leads by your partner, making these offs safe. There is one other problem, though, the missing 6-3 trump. If it is held by one of your opponents and is backed up by another trump, then you will lose one trump lead, with the chance of losing some count. If you want to chance that the 6-3 comes in on the first round, or that your partner adds the 5-5 on one of your trump leads, then you could bid up to 32 – if not, then you should not bid over 31.

[41]

'Strong Trump Hand'

This hand can be played straight through to the 2-1 off and you will have caught every trick. However, if all of the count has come in, then it comes down to who will catch the final trick. If there is a 5 or 10 counter still out at this time, then it is a more serious situation. Either way, we can see that this is not a lay-down hand, and can range from a loss of 1 point to as much as 16 points on just the final play. However, we must not forget randomness, dominos distribution, and your partner's part in the hand. Thus, one could easily bid a mark on this hand if that was needed to obtain bid and feel pretty good about your chances.

Doubles Trump bid

This is a very good doubles trump hand with a slight 'gotcha'. Who has the 5-5? If the 5-5 comes in on the first trump trick, then it is a lay-down at that point as the 6-5 becomes the high domino of the 6 suit by the time it is played, and it being played, in turn makes the 5-4 high in the 5 suit. If you want to gamble that the 5-5 is not backed up by another double and held by one of your opponents, then bid a mark or more to get the bid. If the 5-5 does not fall on the first trick, then you can technically lose as much as 21 points! Since there are only 2 trumps not held by you, the odds that they are both held by one of your opponents is low, which are pretty good odds. If you still do not want to gamble, then bid no more than 31, assuming you will lose the 5-5.

Follow Me bid

This is an example of a pretty strong Follow Me hand as it is clear sailing until the 3-2. We have to assume that several higher 3's will have come in by this time, and there is opportunity for this to happen. For instance, the 6 suit plays could pull in the 6-3, and the 5-5 lead could pull in the 5-3. Of course, the 3-3 will pull in one or more additional. So by the time the 3-2 is played, it could walk or the 4-3 may be held by your partner. If it is taken by your partner, then he may have one or two leads so you can dump the remaining offs. If the 3-2 walks, then the 3-1 will also, bringing you to the 2-1 off lead. Of course, the wheels could fall off on this lead if the dominos fall right, e.g. an opponent has a higher 2 and the other opponent has count. There is a good chance, though, the worst damage would be a loss of 6 points since you have already played the 5-5 and there would be a good chance that the 6-4 would fall during the two 6 suit leads you open with.

Small End Lead bid

This hand falls under the 'strong trump' hand definition above. However, if the bid was won by a bid where you cannot afford to lose a 10 counter trick, namely the 5-5, then the 5-4 is problematic. If the 5-4 is played on the last play of the hand, then it could possibly draw the 5-5 if it is still out.

The solution is to declare 6 as trumps, and lead out the 5-4 but declaring a small end lead, i.e. the 4 suit. Since the 6-4 is in the trump suit and you also have the 4-4, the 5-4 is now the highest 4 and so if it draws out the 4-1 it will catch the trick. After this round, it is a lay-down hand.

This is not an absolute foolproof maneuver though – both defensive players may be void in 4s, one tosses in a trump and the other tosses in the 5-5. But with four 4s held by the other three players, the odds are in your favor.

Nello

'Doubles High'

If we have a hand with the double(s) having a backup in their respective suits, then standard, or Doubles High, would be the call to make. In the above hand we see that we have the almost requisite domino, the 1-0, we have a 2-2 double that is backed up by the 2-0. We have what would be a bad off, the 5-3 but it is backed up by the 3-1 and 5-0. These dominos in turn are backed up by the 1-0. The last domino, the 0-0 double is a walker as there is no 0 lead possible to draw it. If you draw this hand, and you are eligible, then bid Nello.

'Doubles Low'

If you have a double or doubles in your hand and no others of that suit, then you should consider a Nello with Doubles Low bid. In the above hand we see that we have two doubles that are not backed up, the 4-4 and the 1-1. You have a few traditional Nello dominos, the 1-0, 2-1, and 3-1. The downside to a Doubles Low bid is that this is the only time that a 0 lead can draw the 0 suit and not catch it. For instance, the normally 'safe' domino, the 1-0 can set you if a 0-0 is led by one opponent and the other opponent is void in 0's. This would also be the case with the 3-1 and 2-1 except these are backed up with the 1-1 which is the lowest 1 suit. The final domino, the 4-3 is an off that can set you if an opponent led two 4's or 3's and the other opponent was void in either. Even though it is a risk, the odds are that there would be a 6 or 5 lead soon and you, being void in those suits, could dump it. This hand is certainly a playable Nello hand and should be bid as such if given the chance.

'Doubles Catch
Doubles'

Doubles catch Doubles is an interesting Nello variation as it can be successfully played if you have a hand with a mix of high and low doubles that are not backed up by good enough dominos of their suits. In this variation, doubles are their own suit, and so are not drawn out by any other domino of a suit – only other doubles. Examining the above hand, we see that we have three doubles, the 6-6, the 1-1, and the 0-0. We also have a good variety of traditional Nello dominos, the 1-0, 2-1, 2-0. We also have an off, the 5-2. However, following a 5 lead, this domino would still be low and may skate unless opponent two was void in 5's. The 6-6 is backed up by the two lower doubles, the 0-0 and 1-1 so it should be fine unless one opponent had the 2-2, 3-3, and 5-5 and played them all. This would make your 6-6 setting you, but this happening would be probabilistically rare. You should lead out with the 0-0 which would draw 1 or 2 doubles of the 2-2, 3-3, 4-4, or 5-5 selection. If any double was lead back, then you are still protected with the 1-1. The first 6, 4, or 3 lead, dump the 5-2. This is a winnable Nello hand.

Sevens bid

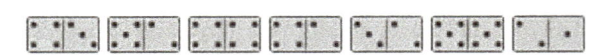

If the dominos are randomly distributed, then this should be a winning Sevens hand. Referring to the distribution chart in the Variations chapter, we can see that the greatest danger point is the sixth play as it follows one play with a 2-point difference and there are five of these. Consequently, if the 1-point difference and 2-point difference dominos are stacked in an opponent's hand, then he could take the sixth play trick. If you get past the sixth trick, then you should win the hand. Sevens requires a one or two mark bid, so you cannot lose a single trick.

Plunge or Splash bid –

There is nothing unique about the hand and any playing strategy with Plunge or Splash except for the doubles requirements to call each respectively. Once the trump is chosen, then play will progress as in any Basic 42 scenario.

As can be seen from the previous section, bidding strategy is a critical part of the game and gets your team started in a strong position or a weak one. Leveraging a proper bid based upon these points, with the following **Offensive Strategy** removes much of the randomness from the hand, and *over time*, will consistently put you in the win column.

Offensive Strategy

Offensive strategy covers that part of the game after the bid is won and the bid-winning team begins play. Offensive strategy focuses on all of the plays that enhance the bidding teams chance to make their bid points and preventing the defensive team from setting them. The strategic points we will examine from the perspective of the Declarer are (Basic 42 only):

- Determining the trump distribution around the table, but especially the partner's trump inventory,
- Play to safely cast off any off(s) on hand and transfer next lead to partner,
- Targeting 'count' dominos to make bid total,
- Properly handling any 'walkers' in the hand,
- Leveraging the partner's hand.

Offensive strategy from the perspective of the bid winner's partner adds these points:

- Properly transmitting the trump inventory of the partner's hand if applicable,
- Playing the correct lead after the declaring partner's 'off' play,
- Adding count to the trick.

If the offensive team, both Declarer and partner, can effectively utilize these strategies, then the randomness of the game can be greatly reduced. This, over time, will make the offensive team the winning team.

Declarer's Strategies

Determining the trump distribution around the table, but especially the partner's trump inventory,

The outstanding trump inventory is a matter of the total of 7 minus what you hold in your hand. The distribution odds are that the remainder is equally divided among the three other players. The trump inventory becomes simple if only one of the remaining players follows your opening trump lead. It is also easy if there are three outstanding trumps and each of them are played by the three other players on the opening play. Where it gets more complex is if only two players follow the opening trump lead. If those players are both on the defensive team, then we know that the remaining trump(s) are held by the defense, but we do not know if they are held by the player upstream from Player 3 (partner) or downstream. This is important only from your partner's view as it can determine the timing to dump counter on the trick. If you only hold three trumps and each player follows your opening trump lead, then you know that there is one remaining trump, but you will not know who holds it. If only two players follow the trump lead, then one of those players has the two remaining trumps, or both of them hold another trump each. If your partner is the only one following your opening trump lead, then we know that all trumps are held by the offensive team, life is good, and the play can be adjusted accordingly.

Play to safely cast off any off(s) on hand and transfer next lead to partner

If you are the Declarer, there will come a point where you cannot maintain the lead and must pass it to someone else. Hopefully, that person will be your partner who may be able to catch a trick or two and allow you to dump any dangerous offs. The off you select to lead should pass the following criteria:

- Not be a 6,5 or 4 if possible (see below)
- Not be a walker (do inventory)
- If your partner has also bid, what has he been casting off during play – has there been several consecutive dominos from the same suit?

The first two criteria are obvious, but the last one may need some explanation. Let's assume your partner has opened the game with a 30 bid but you have overbid him because you have a pretty good hand. This means, unless it was not a Basic 42 hand bid, he will have several good dominos of one suit. If he has followed trumps for a round or two, and thrown in perhaps a counter, what is he casting off? If there are 2 dominos of the same suit going from lower count to higher, then that may indicate his bidding trump suit. This would mean that if he has a quantity of this suit, the remaining players will have few of them. If you have an off of this suit, then play it – you will have a better chance for him to pick up the lead.

One of the most frustrating situations to get into is to have a good hand with only one off – that off being able to draw damaging count, and having no way to get out of the lead so you can dump the off. To prevent this happening, it is best to purposefully lose a trick early by playing a low trump if possible. If you play your high trumps in a row and draw in the mid-value ones, then your lowest trump will walk, you'll catch all of your double leads and then be faced with the bad off on the last trick – a completely random event. Remember, we do not want to leave any play to randomness!

Targeting 'count' dominos to make bid total

The first order of business after you have won your bid is to determine what counters and trick numbers you must capture to make your bid total. Obviously, the 10 counters, the 6-4 and 5-5 are very critical to target. If your bid is 32 or higher, then you cannot afford to lose a trick containing a 10 counter. To protect yourself from a 10 counter loss, then you must be careful to not lead out any suit that can draw these counters. These suits are the 6, 5 and 4 unless your lead is higher. In the case of the 5-5, there are no higher of the suit, so it is especially important to not lead a 5 suit off that may draw it. The exception would be if you strongly felt that your partner may be void in 5's but still have a trump. In this case you would use the 5 suit lead to attempt to draw this counter. The other 10 counter, the 6-4, can be drawn by either a 6 or 4 suit lead making it the most susceptible to 'fishing expeditions' by the opponents. Fortunately, there are several higher in these suits that may catch the trick. Just be sure that you have tracked where these may reside.

Properly handling any 'walkers' in the hand

Offs that remain in your hand at the end-game phase can become powerful plays if they are played at the right time. Proper inventorying of the suits of offs you may have can determine which one to play so that it cannot be caught. If an off can walk because the other 6 dominos of that suit are already in, then the count value becomes moot as it is always the highest of the suit. Don't play offs carelessly just because they do not seem to differ from each other!

Leveraging the partner's hand.

If your partner becomes void in trumps on the first round, then he should throw on count if he has it. If he does, then you should play another trump round to give him opportunity to throw any more count, or, if he is now void in count, a bad off. If during the first round, he is the only one following the trump, then with the trumps in your hand, and what has already been played, you know the trump inventory in his hand. You may then want to first play your double leads (he will throw offs), and then your off in a suit that has the highest number played. This may allow him to trump in if count falls in the trick. He then can reciprocate if possible until what is left are the trump leads. The ideal play from partner-to-partner is that they play the trumps necessary for the Declarer to ascertain the remaining trump inventory, the Declarer to play his doubles (or highest), pass play to his partner who can then play any doubles or highest ranking domino he may have and pass it back to the Declarer for a final trump round. If you and your partner get rolling along like this, then you become almost unstoppable!

Partners Strategies:

Properly transmitting the trump inventory of the partner's hand if applicable

The opening trump round, in many instances, is the Declarer's inventorying opportunity. Unless he has a straight trump set from double to the next three highest trumps, he uses the first round to gain a picture of who has trumps and which ones they have. If you hold more than two trumps and you, as partner, and at least one of the defensive players play trumps on the opening round, then which one you play can be important. As an example, you may hold the next highest trump and a low one – the defensive player having a mid-value one. Playing the high and holding the low trump goes against instinct as you would normally reason that between the two of you, you have the straight line of trumps from the double down for several

[47]

counts. But, the Declarer is concerned where the next highest trump lies. If you do not play it, then he does not know if it is held by you or the defensive player, and, his second highest trump is effectively not high. To show how this works, let's examine the following hands for a few rounds:

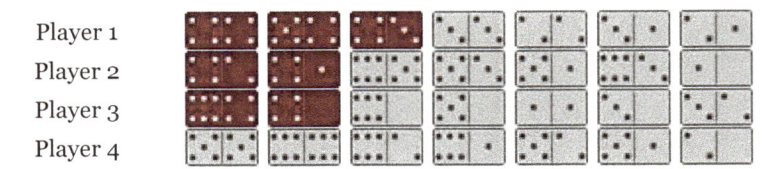

| Player 1 |
| Player 2 |
| Player 3 |
| Player 4 |

We see that the Declarer has three high trumps, the 4-4, 4-5, and 4-3 plus good supporting doubles. What is missing is the 6-4, a 10-point counter. He hopes that it is held bare by one of the other players. His partner, Player 3, holds the 6-4, and also another trump, the 4-0. He may reason that it is a waste to play the 6-4 on the 4-4 when it might be more useful later in the hand, and so plays his low trump instead. Player 1 starts the hand with the 4-4. Here is the hand after the first trick:

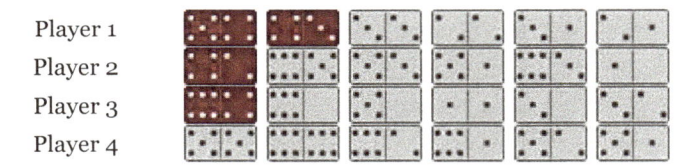

| Player 1 |
| Player 2 |
| Player 3 |
| Player 4 |

Player 1 now has a problem – where is the 6-4? Since both Player 2 and Player 3 both followed the trump lead, it has to reside in either of their possessions. If Player 2 holds it and Player 1 leads his next trump, then Player 4 may dump count on the trick. Fearing this scenario, Player 1 opts to lead an off so as to get out of the lead – his 3-1. Player 2 now follows with his 6-3, Player 3 has to follow with his 3-0 and Player 4 gleefully throws the 5-5 counter, setting the offensive teams' 32 bid.

This scene takes place because Player 3, by playing his low trump, did not transmit needed information to his partner. If Player 2 played his 6-4 on the opening trick, then Player 1 would play differently at this point:

| Player 1 |
| Player 2 |
| Player 3 |
| Player 4 |

Player 1 now knows that he has the highest outstanding trump, the 5-4, and leads it out:

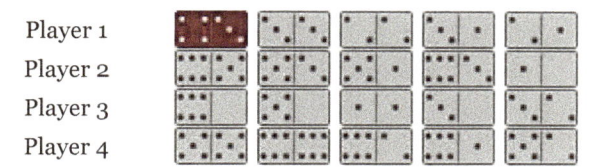

Player 1
Player 2
Player 3
Player 4

Player 1 now plays his two doubles leads leaving these hands:

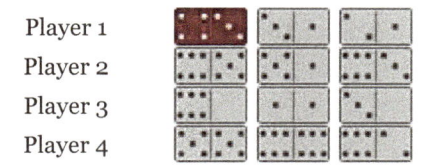

Player 1
Player 2
Player 3
Player 4

Player 1 now chooses to lead his first off, the 2-1. Player 2 throws his 5-1 off, Player 3 adds his 3-0 off, and Player 4 takes the trick with his 6-2. The hand now looks like this:

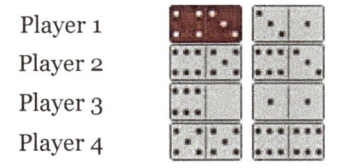

Player 1
Player 2
Player 3
Player 4

Player 4 knows the only counter out is his 5-5 and that Player 1 has a remaining trump. Whether Player 4 plays the 5-5 next or the 6-6, Player 1, since he follows, will on either play have the opportunity to catch the 5-5.

While it is reflexive for the Declarer's partner to want to hold the most valuable trumps for last and play the lowest on a Declarer's high trump lead - from the above example, we can see that it can be detrimental to the Declarer's game-plan. The worst position for Player 1 to be is to be kept in the dark about the trumps distribution.

Playing the correct lead after the declaring partner's 'off' play

In most cases, there will be a point where the Declarer ends his initial trump leads, possibly a double or two, and then must play his low off. Or, he may strategically lead out an off earlier. Hopefully, in any case, if you are his partner, you will catch this lead. This is your part in the hand, and so it is important that you make the most of the action so as to relieve your partner for a trick or two. If you are successful, then there is a good chance you will make your bid. But, what will be a good lead to play after this play? There are several criteria; 1) it should be the highest domino of a suit still in play, 2) it should not present an opportunity for anyone to trump in if there are still trumps out, 3) it should present an opportunity for the Declarer to throw another off if it is required. First, inventory where your playable candidates stand in the suit totals – play the one with the least number played. This can help ensure that the lead is followed and not trumped. If all trumps are in, then play your highest domino that can draw count such as the 6-6, 4-4, 3-3, or 2-2. If you have the 5-5, then most definitely play it – just be sure trumps are in!

Adding count to the trick

Obviously, like the other players, you must follow the Declarers trump lead. However, within one or two rounds, you will become void in trumps, and, if you have count, can add count to the hand so as to help make your team's bid. You should add count only if the Declarer plays trumps that are high, or doubles or the highest ranked domino if trumps are all in or in possession of the Declarer. If you have a 10 counter and 5 counters, then you should always play the 10 counter first, otherwise you will signal your partner that you do not have any 10 counters. If you have both the 6-4 and the 5-5, then you should play the 6-4 first. There are two reasons for this; first, the 5-5 is the highest of the suit and if a 5 is lead, then it can catch it, second, playing the 6-4 early nullifies more leads that would normally draw it (the 6-3, 6-2, 6-1, 6-0, 4-5, 4-3, 4-2, 4-1, 4-0), and there are more that can catch it (the 6-6, 6-5, 4-4). In essence, all but the 4-1 counter become potential offs. The first 5 counter you should play after the 10 counter(s) would be the 5-0 if you have it, then the 4-1 and finally the 3-2. In summary, if you had all of the counters, the order you should play them is: 6-4, 5-5, 5-0, 4-1, 3-2.

Defensive Strategy

Defensive strategy covers that part of the game after the bid-winning team begins play. Defensive strategy focuses on all of the plays and decisions that enhance the non-bidding teams chance to 'set' the offensive team, thus gaining a 'mark' for themselves. Remember, as previously explained, the bid winning team has an advantage, so it is important to carefully analyze the tricks played so as to most successfully leverage your defensive moves. The strategic points we will examine from the perspective of the defensive team are (Basic 42 only):

- Bidding,
- Hiding your trump inventory,
- Hands void of trumps,
- Lead following practices,
- Target counters to 'set' the offensive team,
- Tracking what has been played that matters,

Bidding

A team's players should observe, as the game progresses, if either player of the opposing team is overbidding his hand – and if so make an effort to force him to gain a high bid, and then concentrate on setting him. For more on bidding strategy see the advanced strategy section, page 80.

Hiding Trumps

There is not too much opportunity to hide trumps except at the beginning of the hand and you happen to have more than one trump and Player 3 has at least one. As an example, let's assume trumps are 3's and Player 1 is missing the 3-3, 3-2, and 3-0 (he has the 3-6, 3-5, 3-4 and 3-1). You have the 3-3 and 3-2 and Player 3 has the 3-0. Normally you would trump in with the double trump and lead back with a double. But what if you did not have a good return lead? You should then play the counter trump on the first round. Player 1 may think, since you had to play the counter, Player 3 has the double and misplayed the 3-0. If he then comes back with a lead that can draw a 10 counter and you are void in that lead, then you can now trump in and catch it.

Trump Void Hand

If you find that after trumps are declared your hand is void, then you will need to concentrate on playing the leads and counters you may be left with. After the first trump round, you will have a good idea which players have trumps. Hopefully your partner stays in that group. However, once trumps have been played, and the bidding team has not made their bid, then the playing of your counters and offs is your only hope. Do not blindly follow a lead suit, but if you have more than one domino of that lead suit, play the one that the other end suit has more in play. In other words, you want to be void in as many suits as you can so that you have the opportunity to be able to play count if your partner gets the lead. If you are trapped into always following leads, it diminishes your play options.

Lead Following Practices

Most experienced players play a lead suit only once unless trumps are in and they have several of the highest dominos in that suit. If a non-trump lead is played, then you should play the lowest count value for that suit as long as it is not a counter. There is a special consideration if you have several dominos in that suit – inventory what suits are still un-played and if the suit on the other end of the domino is relatively un-played then do not play this one. It may be a trick catcher on a later lead. To illustrate: Player 1 leads a 6-6 and you hold the 6-3 and 6-1. Which 6 should you play? Looking at the played tricks on the table, you see that five 1's have been played including the 1-0, but only three 3's excluding the 3-1 and 3-0. You should then play the 6-1 as the 6-3 is now high if the 3-2, 3-1 or 3-0 is led later.

Targeting Counters for Setting

After the bidding is over and the bid winner is determined, the defensive team should mentally compute what mix of counter(s) and tricks are required to set the offensive team. For assistance, this table shows what it requires to set the bid-winner:

Bid	Points to Set	Minimum Tricks-Counters combinations to set
30	13	3 tricks with 2 having a 5 counter, 3 tricks with 1 having a 10 counter, 3 tricks with two 5 counters, 1 trick with a 5 counter and a 10 counter
31	12	2 tricks, each with a 5 counter 2 tricks, one with a 10 counter
32	11	1 trick with two 5 counters, 1 trick with a 10 counter
33	10	1 trick with a 10 counter, 1 trick with two 5 counters
34	9	1 trick with a 10 counter, 1 trick with two 5 counters
35	8	1 trick with a 10 counter, 1 trick with two 5 counters, 3 tricks, with 1 having a 5 counter
36	7	1 trick with a 10 counter, 1 trick with two 5 counters, 2 tricks, with 1 having a 5 counter
37	6	1 trick with a 10 counter, 1 trick with a 5 counter
38	5	1 trick with a 10 counter, 1 trick with a 5 counter, 5 tricks – no counters
39	4	1 trick with a 10 counter, 1 trick with a 5 counter, 4 tricks – no counters
40	3	1 trick with a 10 counter, 1 trick with a 5 counter, 3 tricks – no counters
41	2	1 trick with a 10 counter, 1 trick with a 5 counter, 2 tricks – no counters
42	1	1 trick – period!

Figure 9 Bid Setting Table

Obviously, the defensive team catching one or two tricks containing the 6-4 or 5-5 and the 5-0, 4-1 or 3-2 will set any bid. Also catching any trick containing a 5 counter sets any bid from 37 on up. That is why you don't often see bids in the range 37-41 as any counter will set it. That is also why a bid of 36 for a strong trump hand is a good choice as the team can lose a trick with a single 5 counter and make their bid, whereas the other team, having to bid 37 to gain the bid can more easily be set.

Tracking What Has Been Played That Is Important

During the course of the game tracking the counters is an obvious step. However, the defensive team must also track the trump count and dominos that are leads candidates. Tracking the leads is often overlooked as it is more difficult to do during a fast paced game. But, lead inventory tracking can be very beneficial during the end-game phase as it can allow the defensive team to target any remaining count that is out that may help them set the offensive team. In summary you need to track the following, in order of importance:

- Trumps
- Counters
- Leads

Of course, if all of the players see that enough counters have come in for the offensive team to make its bid, then remaining play is a moot point and the remaining dominos can be turned up, ending the hand.

Variations Strategy

There are numerous strategies for the variations described in the chapter on Variations. We will cover each of the following:

Small End Lead -

The small end lead, if allowed by the rules, may be used for only the initial move by the winning bidder. The reason for utilizing a small end lead is for the bidder to throw off an undesirable domino from his hand with the least chance of damage. The reason it is more successful at the opening move is because this is when most dominos are in play. Remember, the ranking rules state that any lead other than a trump is always the highest end of the domino. Thus, to play a small end lead, the bidder must declare the trumps suit, but lead off with a non-trump lead. So that the lead is not determined by the high end, he declares that this lead is the 'small end'. To understand how a small end lead can work, let's take a glance at the following sample hand:

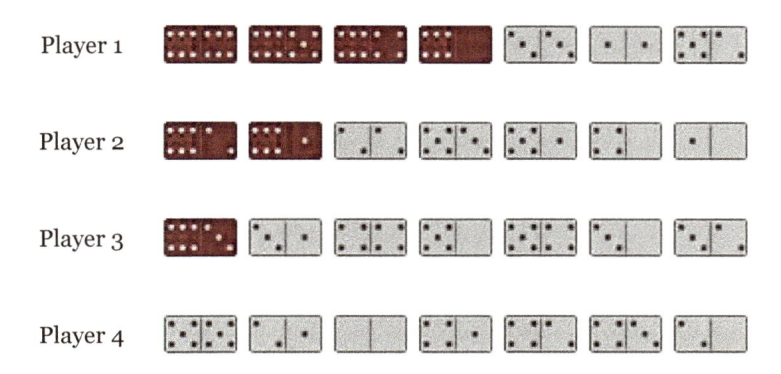

Player 1

Player 2

Player 3

Player 4

Examining the hands, we see that the bid-winner, Player 1, has selected 6's trumps and has four. With the two doubles, the 3-3 and 1-1, he has almost a lay-down hand. Almost, that is, except for one pesky off, the 5-2. This off can possibly draw out the 5-5 if it is still in play on the last round. He needs to be rid of this off, but he has no way to get his partner in the lead. However, Player 1 does have a solution – he can name trumps 6's and lead out the 5-2 as a small end lead.
This lead is played as a 2 suit. Player 2 follows this 2 suit lead with the 2-2 (catching it), Player 3 has to play the 3-2 counter, and Player 4 must follow suit with an off, the 2-0. The end result is that Player 1 loses 6 points, but catches all of the others, making his bid.

Dangerous offs are dominos with 6, 5 or 4 on one end and a smaller count on the other. These can draw the 10 counters and also a couple of 5 counters. If your offs inventory has any of these dominos and you do not have the counters, then be open to a small end lead play.

There are some psychological nuances present with small end leads. All of the players will know the small end lead is an attempt to dump his dangerous off, and by looking at the large end, they will know what counter Player 1 is concerned about. Player 2 may have a counter in the lead suit, or if void has the choice to toss on count. However, he has an opposing player, number 3 following him so he cannot risk casting large count unless he feels that Player 1 will lay-down after dumping this off, and so, may elect to roll the dice and toss in high count. That is not the case with Player 4, however. He is witness to all of the previous plays, and if able, will catch the trick and-or load high count on it.

Be aware that small end leads, as illustrated above have a purpose. Whether you are the defensive team or the partner, by analyzing this lead, you can surmise much.

Nello –

Since the means of winning a Nello hand is to avoid catching a single trick, the hand must generally be a very poor hand, i.e. a 'junk' hand to start. However, unlike the typical junk hand a playable Nello hand can have counters and other normally damaging dominos – as long as they are not *forced* to be played. Reviewing the previous Variations section on Nello, we know only the bid-winner and the defensive team play their hands – the normal bid-winner partner must lay his dominos face down and silently observe the proceedings. In essence, a four domino round now becomes a three domino round. Another factor is that there are no trumps. This means that *all leads* are the big end of the domino.

With this in mind let's analyze the dominos (for illustration you are Player 1, Player 2 is the defensive player on your left, and Player 4 is the defensive player on your right – Player 3 is your non-participating partner):

Dominos that would be considered pretty safe for the Declarer to hold if all dominos were in play:

6-1,6-0,5-1,5-0,4-1,4-0,3-1,3-0,2-1,2-0,1-0

However, these dominos can become liabilities if the defensive team has the right lead (your small end), and you are void in backup dominos. To illustrate, observe the following table:

Dominos You May Hold	Player 2 plays	Player 4 plays
6-0,5-0,4-0,3-0,2-0	0-0 (dbls low)	1-0 or Off
6-1,5-1,4-1,3-1	1-0	2-1,Off or 1-1 (dbls low)
6-2,5-2,4-2,3-2	2-0	2-1,Off or 2-2 (dbls low)
6-3,5-3,4-3	3-0	3-2,3-1,Off or 3-3 (dbls low)
6-4,5-4	4-0	4-3,4-2,4-1,Off or 4-4 (dbls low)
6-5	5-0	5-4,5-3,5-2,5-1,Off or 5-5 (dbls low)

Figure 10 Nello Setting Table

From this table we can see that if you are holding any of the dominos in the 'you may hold' column and the defensive team plays the dominos listed, you will go set. The key is to have a backup for as many of these dominos you can so as to not be forced to follow a lead with your small end but have a high count end.

For example, if you held the 5-1, then a 1-0 lead with the other defensive player throwing an off or any 1 suit with less pips than 5, would make your 5-1 high and you would take the trick. So if you held the 1-0, then it would prevent you catching a 1 suit lead unless doubles were low and if that was the case, then the 1-0 would back up the 5-1. If you held a 4-2, then having the 2-1 or 2-0 would be a good backup as the odds would be that even in a doubles low lead of the 2-2, the other defensive player would hold a higher 2 than the 2-1 or 2-0.

To summarize backup choices for your small end, examine this table:

Dominos You May Hold	Backups (dbls high or own suit)	Backups (dbls low)
6-5	5-4,5-3,5-2,5-1,5-0	5-5
6-4,5-4	4-3,4-2,4-1,4-0	4-4
6-3,5-3,4-3	3-2,3-1,3-0	3-3
6-2,5-2,4-2,3-2	2-1,2-0	2-2
6-1,5-1,4-1,3-1,2-1	1-0	1-1
6-0,5-0,4-0,3-0,2-0,1-0	None	0-0

Figure 11 Nello Domino Backups

It becomes obvious that the 1-0 is the most valuable domino for a Nello hand as it can back up 10 other dominos (the 6,5,4,3,2 with either a 1 or 0 on the small end). (The exception is if doubles are low – then a 0-0 or 1-1 is lower than the 1-0. This does not make the 1-0 valueless, however – it is still a must domino to have). You should have at least two of the following, the 1-0, 2-0, and the 2-1. If you elect to declare doubles low, then any of the doubles can back up their respective suits. Another reason the 1-0 or the 2-0 is valuable is if you hold it and are on the defensive team it can draw out 6 higher dominos and so is an excellent lead.

There is also another factor – not all of the dominos are in play. Remember 25% of the dominos dealt are held face-down by your partner. This means some of the above 'safe' dominos may not be if only 75% of the dominos are in play. As an example, let's say you play the first play with a pretty safe 5-1. Player 2 plays his 5-0 (he has 3 higher 5 suits), the other 5's are held by your partner, Player 3, Player 4 plays an off, and you catch the trick.

The good news is that the laws of probability are in your favor – there are seven dominos in the suit. The odds of any one player being void in the suit are high, while the odds of all of the required dominos being held by the 3 players playing is 3 in 4.

Some considerations from the declarer's perspective:

> a Nello hand can have a high domino of a suit so long as there is a low backup
>
> if you are dealt a number of doubles and you have one or two low, then consider a 'doubles low' declaration. However, examine the following Walker Odds Table – you do not want your doubles to walk!

The effect of walkers -

The danger always present is that a low domino may walk. This is only a danger to *you* on your *opening* play. Any subsequent walker played is only a danger to the defensive team as they catch the trick (good deal for you though). As a rule, you should lead out with the *domino suit that you have the least of*, as long as it is low enough to be safe. Why is this? It is because you are again dealing with the probability of the remaining dominos of the suit being spread so that your opening lead does not 'walk'. As an illustration, if you held all 7 dominos of a suit – any domino you played would walk as there would be none of that suit held by any other player. The following table illustrates this danger:

# of dominoes of suit in your hand	# of dominoes of suit in 3 other hands	% probability held by partner	% probability held by opponents
1	6	2 in 7	4 in 7
2	5	1.66 in 7	3.33 in 7
3	4	1.33 in 7	2.66 in 7
4	3	1 in 7	2 in 7
5	2	.66 in 7	1.33 in 7

Figure 12 Nello Walker Odds Table

We can see from above that if you held 5 dominos of any suit, that the odds of your opponents *together* having any one of the 2 remaining ones is 1.33 in 7 – not too good.

Some considerations from the defensive team's perspective:

> if a lead that either partner plays walks, then that suit is out of play
>
> most players have only one backup for a risky domino – if the declarer follows a lead, you had only two, and your partner played an off, then consider playing your second of that suit if it is low (table above)

What makes up a good Nello hand? Let's analyze a few with each of the three different doubles declarations:

[58]

Hand #1 [dominoes shown] (doubles high)

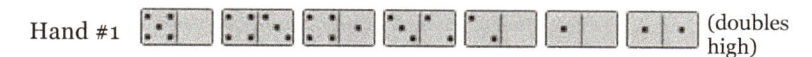

Doubles high means that doubles are treated as they would normally be in a suit, that is, the highest ranked domino of the suit.

This hand contains two moderately dangerous offs, the 4-3 and the 3-2. The 4-3 is backed up by the 4-1 but there is no backup to the 3-2. So if one of your opponents leads a 3-1 or 3-0 and the other player is void in the 3 suit, you will go set. However, you should be able to throw off the 3-2 on the first lead that you do not have to follow (6 for instance). The next caste-off would then be the 4-3. The 1-1 is backed up by the 1-0, but it should be dumped as soon as possible in case an opponent comes back with a second 1 suit lead, making your 1-1 high and catching the trick.

You should lead out with the 5-0 which would then leave you void in 2 suits, the 5 and 6. This increases your opportunity to dump your offs on subsequent plays.

Hand #2 [dominoes shown] (doubles low)

Doubles low means that a double is the lowest domino of a suit, being below the n-0 domino.

In this hand you hold the 2 lowest 6's, the 6-0 and 6-6. You also have the lowest 2, the 2-2 and the 2 lowest 1's, which can back up the 5-1 and the 3-1 if a 1 suit is led.

Again, you should lead out the lowest domino that you have the least quantity of, helping your chances of it not walking on the opening play. This is the 2-2.

On any lead played by the opposing team that you do not have to follow, you should throw off the 5-1 and 3-1 first.

A Nello doubles low declaration is a powerful option. How? To illustrate, say you are Bidder 4, holding the following dominos; 5-5, 4-4, 3-3, 2-2, 3-2, 2-1 and the 1-0. At first glance, this looks like an almost perfect 'doubles' trump hand, except for the missing 6-6. One could risk a 30 bid on a doubles trump call, but it could be dicey as the 6-4 being out and the 3-2 off can be dangerous. But, what about a Nello call with doubles low? Now you have a pretty good hand as the 5-5,4-4,3-3 and 2-2 are lowest of their respective suits, the 1-0 is next lowest, and the 3-2 has three backups, the 3-3,2-2, and 2-1. So, sometimes things are not always as they appear to be!

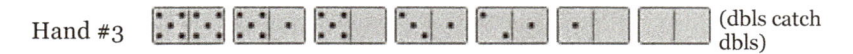

Hand #3 [dominoes shown] (dbls catch dbls)

Doubles catch doubles means that doubles are a suit of their own and are not the highest domino of a suit.

Here, the 5-5 is backed up with the 0-0 and the 5-0 is backed up by the 1-0. The 3-1 and 2-1 have only two dominos lower in each suit so they have a good probability of being caught.

What to lead?

> The 3-1 should be lead out on the opening play even though there is a 3-0 out. However, six 3's are being held by the other three players of which 1-3 are not in play. From the table above, we can see that the odds are good that this lead will be taken. There are four 5's in the suit spread over 3 other hands of which 1-3 are not in play. This means that the odds of a 5 lead walking is fairly high. The 5's will be thrown off on any 6 or 4 suit lead by the defensive team. Any doubles led you will not catch as you have the lowest double, the 0-0, unless another double is led and you have not thrown off the 5-5.

These examples merely show the technique of probabilities in picking how to bid and play Nello. There will still be randomness in each hand that can sneak in causing you to lose the hand. However, *over time*, good analysis and strategic choices will greatly reduce randomness as a factor.

Also remember, there is no lay-down hand in Nello!

Plunge and Splash –

Plunge and Splash are differentiated only in the bidding and first player identity from the Basic 42 game. Consequently, there is no playing strategy per se, except the offensive team must play to lose no trumps, as both contracts require catching all tricks.

Sevens –

As mentioned under 'Sevens' in the variations chapter, there are limited strategies in a Sevens hand as one must follow with a domino totaling as close to seven pips as possible. However, there are several points we can mention here to help you play a winning Sevens hand.

Recognizing a Sevens hand to bid –

> The major offensive strategy in Sevens is determining when to bid or not to bid on Sevens. Consequently, the bid hand analysis is the most critical part.
>
> First, pips totaling seven do not easily jump out at you from a hand of seven dominos, so it is important to memorize the key dominoes you should hold so as to bid Sevens. You should memorize the three dominoes that total 7, the 6-1, the 5-2, and the 4-3. You should have at least one of these dominoes and preferably two to start. Next, the 8 or 6 total dominoes, the 6-2, 5-3, 4-4, 6-0, 5-1, 4-2 and 3-3 that you should have two of. After this, then you should have any of the 3 and 4 difference dominoes. If it depended only upon your hand, then holding the 6-6 or 0-0 would be a guarantee of being set, but you do have a partner that may be in a position to carry the play if you lead out with a high difference domino. As a practice though, I do not recommend calling Sevens if you are holding the 1-0 and-or the 0-0.

The following table shows the domino's ranks for Sevens, in order of best to worst:

Domino(s)	PIPS Total	Change from 7
6-1,5-2,4-3	7	0
6-0,5-1,4-2,3-3	6	-1
6-2,5-3,4-4	8	+1
5-0,4-1,3-2	5	-2
6-3,5-4	9	+2
4-0,3-1,2-2	4	-3
6-4,5-5	10	+3
3-0,2-1	3	-4
6-5	11	+4
2-0,1-1	2	-5
6-6	12	+5
1-0	1	-6
0-0	0	-7

Figure 13 Sevens Domino Rankings Table

Examining this table, we can observe the following:

- There are only 3 dominos with a 7 total – if evenly distributed these should come in on the first round
- There are 7 dominos with a 1 difference total
- There are 5 dominos with a 2 difference total
- There are 5 dominos with a 3 difference total
- There are 3 dominos with a 4 difference total
- There are 5 dominos with a 5 or higher difference total

It should be noted that because of the rules of play, what you have in your hand may be better than you realize. To illustrate, let's assume you are holding the following hand which you will bid as Sevens:

To see how this hand would play out (assuming random distribution), examine the following chart (you are PL 1):

[61]

P	PL 1	PL 2	PL 3	PL 4	Note
1					2 diff 0's in, 1 diff 1, 1 diff 2
2					All diff 0's in, 3 diff 1's, 1 diff 2, 1 diff 3
3					5 diff 1's in, 2 diff 2's, 2 diff 3's
4					All diff 1's in, 4 diff 2's 2 diff 3's
5					All diff 2's in, 4 diff 3's, 1 diff 4
6					All diff 3's in, 2 diff 4's, 2 diff 5's
7					All diff 4's in, All >diff 4's in

Figure 14 Sevens Play Sequence Example

We can see that although it is technically feasible that the above hand can go set (if the dominos are not distributed evenly), as play progresses it is a race between the Declarer and the rest of the players, with many plays being equal differences (but the Declarer plays first, so he gets the trick).

A good Sevens hand would have at least two 7 totals, 2 or more 6 or 8 totals, and 2 or more 5 or 9 totals. It should not have the 1-0 or 0-0 unless you want to gamble on your partner catching the trick that you lead with either of these dominos.

There is not a defensive strategy against a Sevens call as one must play the domino with the nearest total pips to 7 and hope that you OR your partner has a nearer to seven total than both players of the bid-winning team. The first domino played of a specific total is the one that counts. Obviously, once the bid-winner starts play, if several players count totals equals his, he catches the trick since he has played first. Because of this, the bid-winner has an advantage during play.

Partners Response during a Sevens bid

There is no strategy as a partner in Sevens unless you take the trick from your partner's lead. Then you must lead back out with your closest to a 7 domino. Hopefully, your next lead will be taken by your partner and-or you can continue the leads until the hand is completed.

The strategies we have covered up to this point, if followed, will greatly reduce the ***randomness*** factor in the game, and thus increases the odds that you and your partner, ***over time***, can post a winning record. However, we are not quite finished...

Advanced Strategy

Now that we have covered basic strategies for the different aspects of the game, it is time to address some advanced strategic pointers. Don't be intimidated by the use of logic tables and probabilities as this will be where much of the 'killer 42' stuff will be found!

Once you have played 42 for a while, and have played against some experienced players, you'll notice that some players seem to always know who have certain dominos during the game. While having a photographic memory is a big help in many games, it only helps in 42 if you are stacking tricks in 1 or 2 mark bid games. So, what's their secret? They have learned on their own, **intuitively**, how to use logic and probability techniques to their advantage. They may not even recognize these techniques - they have just learned from experience over many games played.

What I'll try to do here is to explain how to more fully utilize logic and probability to *duplicate* these learned abilities.

We'll touch on three areas of the game; 1) analyzing a drawn hand, 2) analyzing the plays in a trick, and 3) analyzing the end game. To wrap up this chapter, we'll also cover three other aspects, timing, misdirection, and advanced playing tips. (These strategies pertain only to Basic 42 unless otherwise noted).

Analyzing a Drawn Hand

Opening Hand

The most important hand to analyze is the opening hand. The reason is that there are more dominos in play, and a correct analysis (or alternatively, an incorrect one), can set the path for how the rest of the game can progress. What we want to do is determine these points:

- What is the trump distribution and how will they play?
- Which lead(s) do you have that may play a round?
- Where are the counters and how will they fall?
- What dominos qualify as 'walkers?'

Trump Status

To illustrate, let's play through the following hand (Player 1 has won the bid with a bid of 31, table does not show actual plays):

[63]

Player 1 has declared 4 as trump and we can see that he has the 2 high trumps for the first 2 plays. On round 1 he sees that Player 2 follows with a low trump, his partner (3) plays his 4-2 (when he would play the 4-5 if he has it), and Player 4 plays an off. On round 2 all players see that Player 2 plays another trump and Players 3 and 4 play either offs or counters. At this point the trump status has been determined; 5 trumps have been played, and Players 3 and 4 are void. However, only Player 1 and 2 know the status of the remaining 2 trumps since they hold them. Player 1 must, for the remaining tricks, keep Player 2 out of the lead and following his non-trump leads until the last trumps fall. Player 4 must hold his 5-5 until he sees Player 1 having to lead his 4-3 on the last trick or Player 2 leading with the 4-5 trump (either way the defensive team gains the 5-5).

Playable Leads

Continuing with the above hand, we see that Player 1 has two good leads, the 3-3 and the 2-2. Player 2 does not have any good leads unless he knew what his partner, Player 4 held, which he doesn't. Player 3 has the 6-6 and the 1-1 as the only viable leads, and Player 4 has the 5-5, and after the 6-6 falls, the 6-5.

Counters Status

In the above hand, we see that Player 1 has a 10 counter in his trump line-up, Player 2 has the 4-1 counter in his trump inventory, and Player 3 has the 5-0 and 3-2 counters that he will add when he sees that his partner has the high trump. When Player 3 and 4 see the 4-1 fall on the second round, they may falsely assume that Player 2 is void in trumps. Of course he and Player 1 know the truth - that Player 2 now has the high trump (the 4-5) and is in a good position to take a damaging trick. Player 4 has an excellent counter as it is also the high of that suit. He will want to save this lead if possible, until all of the trumps are in.

Walkers Determination

Player 1 has two offs, the 3-1 and 2-1, Player 2 has the 5-3, 5-1, 6-3 and 1-0. Player 3 has the 3-0 and 3-2, and Player 4 has all dominos except the 5-5. Most of these dominos can 'walk' depending upon the play progression. When it gets to the end-game phase and Player 1 is in the lead, he would want to count the number of 3's and the number of 2's to determine whether his 3-1 or the 2-1 would be the better play. Same with Player 2 – he would count how many 5's and 6's are in to determine which one to play. He could play the 1-0 only if all the other 1's were in as it is the lowest of that suit. Player 3, if in the lead, would need to inventory the 6's, 5's and 3's to determine if he has a walker. Player 4 checks the 6's, 5's and 2's so as to determine a possible walker. Remember, the walker will only walk if all trumps are in or being held back.

Analyzing a Drawn hand – Following hands

After the opening hand is played, we have more information as each subsequent hand is played. As play progresses, further information we want to deduct is:

- What is the current counter status?
- If lead is gained, what domino to lead back with?
- If not in the lead, what possible 'setting' dominos to protect?

Let us re-examine the previous hand after two rounds have been played. Player 1 has led his 4-4 on the opening round, and attempting to draw the 4-5 from either Player 2 or 3, leads out round 2 with his 4-6. The following shows the inventory of the hands after the first two rounds:

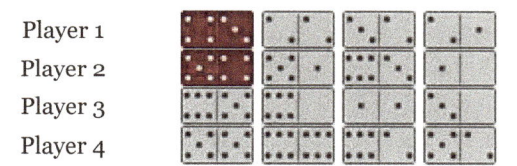

Player 1
Player 2
Player 3
Player 4

Player 1 knows that at this point Player 2 has a higher trump than what he holds and he must hope the remaining 10 counter will fall on the next few plays. He also knows that if he leads his final trump, Player 2 will have to follow trump lead, and there is a chance that Player 4 can drop the 5-5 on the trick. He would also like to save his 3-2 counter as the last lead in hopes that it can walk. So he next leads the 3-3 and then the 2-2 in hope that he can draw the remaining counters from his partner. On the 3-3 lead, Player 2 follows with the 3-5, Player 3 adds the 3-1 and Player 4 throws in the 5-2 or 5-1 off.

The hand now looks like this:

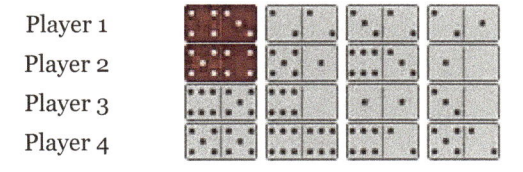

Player 1
Player 2
Player 3
Player 4

On the next round Player 1 leads out the 2-2 and Player 2 being void in 2's has the choice to either trump in or throw an off. He decides it is too early to use his trump since he has a poor choice for a return lead and plays his 1-0 off. Player 3 is void in 2's and adds his 3-0 off. At this point, Player 1 knows that the 5-5 is being held by Player 2 or 4. Player 4 completes the trick by playing his 5-2.

This is the hand inventory now:

Player 1			
Player 2			
Player 3			
Player 4			

On the next round, Player 1 must now lead with his off, the 2-1. Player 2 has no 2's and again decides against trumping at this time, so he plays his off, the 5-1 (voiding himself in the 5 suit). Player 3 has no 2's so plays an off, the 6-0. Player 4 takes the trick with his 6-2.

This is the inventory at the end-game phase:

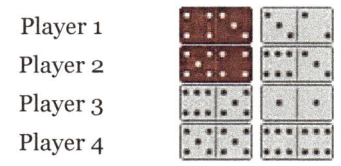

Player 1		
Player 2		
Player 3		
Player 4		

At this point Player 1 starts to feel the heat as he knows that Player 2 holds a higher trump than he (even though Player 3 and 4 do not know), his last off is the 3-2 counter, and the 5-5 is still out. He does not want to have the trumps fall together on the last play as there could also be the 5-5. It would also have been advantageous for this round for Player 2 being the last to play (i.e. Player 3 being first) so that both Player 3 and 4 do not know who will trump in, Player 1 or 2. However, Player 4 does have the lead and has his own quandary – does he lead out with the 5-5 and hope his partner has the higher trump, or save it for the last round? Since Player 2 on the second round played the 4-1 trump he might think that Player 2 is void in trumps, and if that is the case, the two last rounds are moot as Player 1 would take both. With this uncertainty, Player 4 decides to delay the inevitable and save his 5-5 to the last round – so leads his 6-5. Player 1 does not know between Player 2 and 4 who has the 5-5 (he knows Player 3 doesn't as he has played an off earlier). The question is, does he trump in now or wait? He knows if he plays his 4-3 trump now, Player 2 will not trump in, saving his trump for the last play with the 5-5 and 3-2 counters out. He also does not know that Player 2 must follow the 6-5 lead with his 6-3. So Player 1 plays his remaining off, the 3-2 counter in hopes that Player 2 jumps at it, and making Player 1's 4-3 trump good for the final trick. However, Player 2 has to play his 6-3 and so has no chance for the trick, which is taken by Player 3's 6-6. On the final lead, Player 3 leads with his 1-1, Player 4 adds the 5-5, Player 1 trumps in with his 4-3, Player 2 over-trumps with his 4-5 and takes the trick with the 10 counter, the 5-5.

Unfortunately for the defensive team, this one 11- point trick is not enough to set the bid-winners as the bid was 31, allowing a loss of 11 points.

But what if on round 6 Player 4, instead of leading his 6-5, leads out with the 5-5? Now Player 1 has no choice – he must trump in so as to not add his 3-2 counter to the pot for Player 2 to catch. His only hope at this point is that Player 2's final lead will be caught by his partner or himself, thereby keeping the loss to only 11 points and winning the hand. Player 2 knows that his team needs 12 points to set the offensive team, realizes that the 5-5 must not get by and so, over-trumps Player 1. This time, though, Player 2's last domino is the 6-3 which he leads out. Player 3 must follow with his 6-5, Player 3 catches the trick with the 6-6, and Player 1 plays his 5 counter, the 3-2. The defensive team has now collected 17 points and has set the offensive team.

What this analysis shows, is that keeping track of the dominos is very important and the timing of plays is consequential. What a difference the right play at the right time makes!

Analyzing Plays in a Trick

Analyzing each player's play in a trick can telegraph much of what their hand contains. This is especially helpful in determining what your partner may hold, since the two of you playing off of each other may help make a bid, or, prevent the opposing team from making theirs. We will outline these analyses from player position 2 through 4 (position 1 does not analyze as he is the first play).

Obviously, as in bidding strategy, the playing position determines the amount of analysis available, with position 4 having the most information presented. The following table outlines each position's view (opening play of a hand only):

Your Position	Previous Player-Play	Analysis
Player 2	Player 1	
	Trump Double	*Condition:* Normal play for normal trump hand. *Action:* Must follow if you have trump. If you have 2 or more trumps play the lowest value.
	Trump-6	*Condition:* Unless player is messing around or inexperienced, indicates bidder does not have the double trump and feels he can lose a round at the beginning of the hand. Not a good move if trump is 5 or 4 because of possible 10 count loss. *Action:* Same as above unless you have double, then play it and hope your next lead the bidder has, your partner doesn't and throws on high count.
	Trump-1,2	*Condition:* Leading with a low trump is not real common, but works if the Declarer's partner has a fairly high trump and can get into the lead for a round.

			Dangerous in that an opposing team player may also have a higher trump and the 5-5 or 6-6. *Action:* If you have a medium high trump and a low one, play the higher and hope that Player 4 does not trump higher than you. If lead is gained then lead back with a double that can draw count.
		Calls trump, but leads out with another lead.	*Condition:* Indicates that there are some holes in the bidder's trump suit. Bidder may have had bid dropped on him and is trying to flush the weak dominos from his hand. *Action:* If you have a higher lead, then play it and hope it stands so you can get into lead. If you cannot follow lead and have a trump, then trump in but use a low trump and hope other players must follow lead suit. If Player 4 is also void in the lead and can play trump you do not waste your higher trump by being over-trumped by him.
Player 3	Player 2		
		[Player 1] Double Trump.	*Condition:* Player 2 follows with lowest trump *Action:* If you must follow trump lead and your partner has made an aggressive bid, then play your highest trump (so he knows where missing high trump is). If your partner has had a forced bid, then play your lowest trump as you may have to complement his trump suit. If you are void in trumps, then play the highest counter that is not a good lead itself (i.e. the 6-4 instead of the 5-5).
		[Player 1] Trump-6	*Condition:* Player 2 follows with a low trump if able *Action:* The bid winner leading with other than the double, unless known by his partner (you), is not a good lead. If the partner knows that the bid winner partner plays the opening this way, and you do not have the double, then play as normal as the bid winner may be doing a psych number on the other team. If you do have the double play it, so your partner knows where it is and you can get into the lead for a round.
		[Player 1] Trump-1,2	*Condition:* Player 1 is purposely leading with a low trump so as to relinquish the lead for one round at the least damaging time. This usually tells you that he has a bad off(s) and needs to dump it-them ASAP. *Action:* Play the highest trump you can if it is higher than what Player 2 plays. This is in the hopes of getting the lead. Even if you are over-trumped by Player 4 it will draw out the defensive team's higher trump.
		[Player 1] Calls trump, but leads with another lead.	*Condition:* Player 2 follows the lead. *Action:*

			If you are void in the lead played and there have not been any of this suit previously played, then you may consider playing count. If you are not void in the lead suit, then inventory the lead suit in your hand and the two that have been played. If it totals 5 or more, then it would be better to play an off as it is a good chance one of the defensive players may trump in.
Player 4		Player 3	
		[Player 1] Double Trump.	*Condition:* Player 2 and 3 follow the lead. *Action:* If you have trump, you play your lowest. If you are void in trump, then play your lowest off.
		[Player 1] Trump-6	*Condition:* Player 2 and 3 follow the lead. *Action:* If Player 2 plays the double trump and you are void in trumps, then play the highest count possible. If Player 3 plays the double trump, then play the lowest trump if you have trump, otherwise play a low off. If you have the double trump and another trump, then play the lower trump - if only the double is in hand, or if Player 3 throws count then play the double.

Figure 15 Analysis of Plays Table

Analyzing the End-Game

Many times the fate of the hand comes down to the last few rounds. This is because the make or set counters which have been fished for by the offense and hoarded by the defense will now likely fall. This is what we can define as the 'end-game' phase, and for the purpose of this analysis, we will limit to the two last rounds or tricks.

What we would like to know going into this phase is:

- Score Status
- Trump status
- Counters placement
- Likely Lead Inventory
- Walkers status

Score Status

Before we enter the end-game, a player should know by now the score status. That is, how many points are in for each team, how many points are still out and how many points does the bidding team need to make their bid.

Players should count the counters and tricks for both teams for the played total. Naturally that count subtracted from 42 determines what points are still un-played (2 remaining tricks subtracted from this count gives us the counters count still out, itemizing the counters already played gives us the remaining counter dominos). Once we have this picture, we can combine it with prior moves from each player to determine where the counters may be. For example, if the score status shows the 6-4 is still un-played, and Player 1 has lead out previously with the 6-6 and Player 3 has played a 6-2 or so; or Player 1 has played a lead and Player 3 has played an off, then we know that the 6-4 is not held by Player 3. If you are Player 2 or Player 4 and you do not have the 6-4, then you know that your partner or Player 1 can possess it. If you are Player 1 and either Player 2 or 4 has played an off, then you know the other opponent has it. Once the counter inventory is deduced, then the following remaining items should be determined.

Trump Status

It is important to analyze what the trump status is at this point if they are still in play. Sometimes all of the trumps have already come in and thus are not an issue. However, there may still be 1 or 2 out at this point. If this is the case, then it is good odds that only the bidding player will be holding them or they are split between the bid-winner and a defensive player. The exception would be if the bid winner decides to name trump and leads out with a few doubles hoping to draw some count from his partner. This will leave his trumps for the last plays of the hand. A defensive team player may have more trumps, but they may be lower ones. If this scenario takes place, it will be difficult to know where the trumps are, as it will be very similar to the first two rounds of the game where each player must follow suit.

Counters Placement

After the score status is totaled, determining where the remaining counters are located is critical to either making bid or setting the bidding team. The reason for this is by the very makeup of the round rotation and the offense and defense players being alternating. The goal, if you are the offensive team, is 1) for the leading partner to play the lead that will allow his partner to not be able to follow so he is able to dump counter offs on the trick, and 2) prevent the defensive team from playing a higher lead or trumping in to catch it. If Player 1 starts the lead and Player 2 follows with a subordinate lead, then Player 3 may throw count onto the trick and only have Player 4 as a danger to catch it.

There is a factor about counters though that needs to be addressed. Three counters are higher dominos in their suits, one is in the middle and one is low. The following chart illustrates this:

Counter	Explanation
5-5	This counter is the highest domino in the 5 suit. Any other 5 played as a lead, the counter will catch it. The 5-5 is an excellent lead by itself as long as all players must follow the suit (i.e. not trump in).
6-4	If the 6-4 is lead, then it is a 6 suit and the 6-6 and 6-5 can catch it. If the 4-4 has been played, and a 4 suit is led, then the 6-4 is high and can catch the trick.
4-1	If the 4-1 is led, then it is a low 4 suit domino, only catching the 4-0. If the 1-1, 1-6, and 1-5 have been played, and a 1 suit is led, then the 4-1 is high and catches the trick.
5-0	If the 5-0 is lead, then any 5 suit domino can catch it. The 5-0 as a 0 suit, can only be caught by the 0-0 lead as there are none others. This is why this domino is the worst 'off' to lead as it cannot catch anything, and only one 0 suit can draw it, the 0-0. If you are forced to lead it on the last play and there are still 5's out, it is akin to throwing a raw steak to a pack of hungry wolves.
3-2	If the 3-2 is led, then it is a low 3 suit domino, only catching the 3-1 and 3-0. If the 2-2, 2-6, 2-5 and 2-4 have been played, and a 2-1 or 2-0 is led, then the counter is high and can catch the trick.

Figure 16 Counters Suit Rankings

From this chart, it becomes obvious that once a Player determines what counters are in his partner's hand he can leverage that with the correct play so as to have a good chance to catch that counter.

As an example, if any 5 suit is led by a player, and his partner has the 5-5, then they will catch that counter as long as the opposing players cannot trump in. If a player has determined that his partner has a good chance to hold the 6-4 and sees that the 6-6 and 6-5 are already in, then he can lead out a low 6 suit domino and his team will catch that counter. The same holds true for the 4-1 and the 3-2 but there are less subordinate dominos of those suits that may still be in play. Also with these 2 counters, since there are less dominos of the suit that may be in play, then it is important that the trumps be in so that an opposing player does not trump in. Consequently, these 2 counters are best fished for in the end-game phase. The 5-0 will never be the 'catching' domino from a 5 suit lead as it is the lowest 5 suit. However, if all 5 suit dominos but the 5-0 are in, and trumps are in, then this counter can 'walk'.

Likely Lead Inventory

A lead domino is either the double (or the highest un-played) of one of the non-trump suits. During the course of the hand, the inventory of all of these dominos you have in your hand is important. However, the value of this inventory depends upon three things:

- The actual lead domino value

  As mentioned above a lead is defined as the highest playable domino of a suit. Usually it is safest to depend upon doubles only, unless the trumps are in and you are in the end-game phase. If it is end-game, then a tally of the dominos that have been played can easily determine what will be the highest domino.

- The Trumps status

  If all of the trumps are in, then they are not a factor and a double lead is un-beatable. If all of the trumps except one are in, then only a double of a suit that you do not have a quantity of, and few already played should be played. If you have three dominos of the suit in your hand, then there are four remaining dominos distributed among three players, and you have a good chance of being trumped.

- The playing position you have in relation to the Declarer

  This is a subtle part of the leads analyses. To illustrate, let us assume that you have the lead and that you are NOT the Declarer. The three positions you can occupy are:

    o The Declarer on your left (you are Player 4),
    o The Declarer on your right (you are Player 2),
    o The Declarer across from you (your partner – you are Player 3).

  Now let's see how these positions can affect the value of your leads inventory.

  Declarer on left –

  If the bid winner is on your left and you lead, this means that he has two players playing after him, a defensive player and an offensive player, his partner. If the bid winner (who would normally hold the greater number of trumps) is void in your lead suit, then he has a choice of playing an off or trumping in. If your lead is the 5-5 then he would choose to trump in so as to catch the ten-counter. If your lead is the 6-6, 6-5 or 4-4, he also may trump in so as to not chance missing the 6-4. If this happens and Player 2 and 3 has to follow lead and the 6-4 does not fall, then he may have wasted a trump. If you lead with a domino that may draw a five counter, then he may elect to sacrifice it and throw an off so as to clear it from his hand.

  Declarer on right –

  If the bid winner is on your right, that places him as the last to play. This is the most powerful position for him to be in as he then, after seeing what three dominos have fallen, and, being void in the lead suit, has the choice to play a trump or off for maximum effectiveness.

Declarer across (partner) –

This is certainly the most advantageous position for you to be in, and, the most powerful from your part. The reason is that you are making the choice to play a lead to help your partner to make your bid. In this scenario, you should target a lead that has a good chance to be void in your partner's hand. You can determine this by choosing a lead suit that you may have other dominos in, or that have had a number already played. Since your partner would probably have more trumps in his hand than either defensive player, the odds of him being void in the suit is better. If this is so, then he has the option to play an off or a counter such as a 5-0 or 3-2 that may not walk by itself. If he does this, then only Player 4 can be a factor, and then only if he has a trump and is void in the lead suit. If you are the partner to the Declarer and have obtained the lead, it is not a good idea to lead with the 6-6 or 5-5 as either of these leads can lead to a ten-counter loss if either of the defensive players have a trump, are void in 6's or 5's and your partner is not. Target the five-count suits 0-3 for your leads.

As can be seen from above, the value of your leads are 1) most valuable with the Declarer across from you, 2) next valuable with the Declarer to your left, and 3) least valuable with the Declarer on your right. Keeping this in mind, choose your lead carefully.

Walkers Status

A 'walker', as defined earlier, is a domino that when led, cannot be followed by any more dominos of that suit as they have already been played. This naturally makes this domino the highest of its suit and will catch the trick unless a trump is played. Walkers are most effective in the end-game phase when all the trumps are in, or a trump is explicitly not played.

Determining if the remaining dominos in your hand are walkers is simple - you merely inventory how many of those in the suits have been played (6 others played = you have a walker). Unfortunately, if the bid is a mark or more then only the last eight dominos are visible, and you may have to depend upon your memory. If the last two dominos in your hand are a walker and an off, and you have the lead, then play the walker first and throw the off on the last play. This allows your partner to discard a bad off (like the 5-0) and then take the last trick with his remaining trump.

Timing

Greek poet Hesiod exclaimed, *"Observe due measure, for right timing is in all things the most important"*. In many things, including 42, this is sage advice. Where though, does timing apply in the game of 42? We'll examine the following areas:

- When to switch from trumps to leads,
- When to play count,
- When to play offs.

When to switch from Trumps to Leads

This timing issue pertains mainly to the Declarer as most other players' trump run is usually transitory. This decision can be pretty complex as it depends greatly upon your trump count and spread. The easiest way to demonstrate timing is through several sample hands:

Sample #1

You Have...

Here, we have 4's as trumps and you have the two highest plus a lower one. If you play the trumps straight through, followed by the doubles, you should take all tricks until your off, the 5-2. This off, however, is a dangerous one as it can draw the 5-5 and-or the 5-0 on the last play. You very much need to be out of the lead for one round so as to be able to dump this off.

How to play...

You should play the 4-4 first so as to get a read on the trumps distribution. If the only trump played is from a defensive player, then the above scenario is void and you will probably go set unless your partner holds all of the remaining count. If the trumps are scattered however, then your second play should be the 4-2. This trick will now be taken by another player - hopefully by your partner. On the lead-back play, you may be able to now dump the 5-2 and on the next play you will recapture the lead with the 6-4 or one of your doubles and continue your hand.

Sample #2

You Have...

In this example, you have three trumps, two doubles, and two offs, neither that present any high danger.

How to play...

We should not switch to doubles leads until all of the trumps are in as we do not want a rogue trump from a defensive player taking count thrown onto your double lead by your partner. We also do not want to get out of the lead by playing an off next as this can nullify the double leads since an opponent may lead back with leads other than 3's or 2's. After you play the two doubles, then throw your first off, the 2-1. The reason this should be the one played is that one 2 is taken by your trump (4-2), and you have led out a 2's round with your 2-2 double. This may make your 2-1 walk and if it does, then the 6-2 concludes the hand and it is possible it may walk, catching any count held by the defensive team for the last play.

Sample #3

You Have...

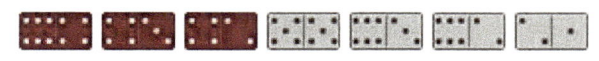

In this example, you have had the bid dropped on you. You have three trumps (4's), a double, and three offs, none that present any high danger. The trumps you have are not necessarily the best you should have to bid this hand. However, you do have a count of 20 points, one being the highest in its suit, and the other being a high trump. The problem you have is that your other trumps are low, and if the remaining trumps are distributed unfavorably, there is the chance that your 6-4 could be caught by the 4-4. Another danger is that your 5-5 is not backed up, and with as many possible trumps being held by others, an opponent may play a 5 lead, drawing out your double 5 with the other opponent trumping in.

How to play...

Your goal is to protect your two 10 counters and play them at the time when you can keep them. There are two ways to play the hand. You can play it fairly conventional and lead out a low trump in the hopes that your partner has the double and another one or so, or, you can play the probabilities. The probabilities are that there are 5 trumps divided among three other players and it is possible that one or both of the defensive players can have enough trumps to catch the 6-4, especially on three tries. There are five other 5's of your 5-5 suit. The odds of no player having a 5 domino at this time are good. So, the math tells us to go for the 5-5 first, and after naming 4's trumps you should lead out with the 5-5. After this trick you then have to go with playing the trumps (4-3 first) so that the last trump lead you are able to catch with the 6-4. If this happens, then you have the three offs remaining, of which two, the 6-3 and 6-2 may catch the trick or walk. Do NOT play the 2-1 at this time as it will guarantee you being out of the lead and negate the two good offs that may walk.

If a defensive player is playing another suit, you will not be able to catch anything if you have dominos that only **you** hold.

Another scenario can be if you catch the second trump lead. You will now hold the 6-4, 6-3, 6-2 and 2-1. If the 4-4 is in, then you should play the 2-1 to give the lead away. On the next plays you can trump back in with the 6-4 and try to walk the other 6(s). If the 4-4 is out, then lead out the 6-3 so as to coerce the 4-4 holder to trump in, and on the next play(s), again, trump in with the 6-4.

When to play Count

The most advantageous time to play count can apply to both the offensive team AND the defensive team. The goal of the offensive team, of course, is to catch enough of the counters to make their bid. Alternately, the defensive team's desire is to catch enough of the count to set their opponents. If the offensive team's hand results in them being in the lead for every trick, then timing the count play is a moot point as they will catch all of it. However, spotty hands, where it is not apparent who will catch what, makes the timing of count play much more critical. The following table lists some choices:

Play	Analysis
Declarer's opening play is a low trump or low off	This normally indicates Declarer has a bad off, and is attempting to get out of the lead for a round so he can throw it. If you are Player 2 there is an offensive player and a defensive player following you – thus, a 50-50 chance that your partner can catch the trick. The odds that you will lose this hand is high if the Declarer slips the bad off(s) by as he will then have a very strong hand remaining. With this in mind, play the highest counter you have.
Declarer leads trumps that are known high	Offensive partner throws count at every opportunity.
Declarer leads a double in suit after trumps are in	Offensive partner throws count if not required to follow lead.
Declarer leads a walker	Offensive partner throws count if trumps are in.
Player 2 catches trump trick, leads double	If Player 3 follows lead, and Player 4 is void, should inventory lead suit and if only 2 or 3 of suit played, throw count onto trick.

Figure 17 When to Play Count Table

When to Play Offs

Offs are the ugly stepchildren for most players and are sometimes treated as 'fillers'. However, knowing what offs to play, and when to play them is a powerful asset and can make a hand go your way or not. The following table shows some sample offs and when they might be played:

Off	Analysis
1-0	This off is the guaranteed 'I want to be out of the lead' off as every 1 suit domino will catch it. If all 1's are already in though, it walks – so inventory before playing – you may want to be out of the lead or not.
2-0, 2-1, 3-0, 3-1	These offs will draw a 5-point counter, the 3-2, if it is still out. If the 3-2 is already in, then these offs can be played.
4-0, 4-2, 4-3	These offs can draw two counters, the 6-4 and the 4-1 so they are especially dangerous if neither of these counters have fallen. If the 6-4 is already in, then the risk is lessened. Better to play at the end-game phase.
5-0, 5-1, 5-2, 5-3, 5-4	Another set of dangerous offs, drawing both the 5-5 and 5-0. Only play these when at least the 5-5 is in and preferably both.
6-0, 6-1, 6-2, 6-3, 6-5	These offs can draw only the 6-4 counter. They should be played only after it has come in.

Figure 18 When to Play Offs Table

As can be seen from the above, keeping track of the 5-5 and 6-4 is critical to deciding which off you select to play.

Misdirection

Misdirection in 42 is the practice of playing certain dominos at particular times to throw off what your opponents deduce about what you may hold in your hand. Much of the previous strategy focuses on determining what players are holding by how they bid and play. Knowing this, using misdirection means to play outside these rules when possible so as to hide or disguise what you may hold. Misdirection should only be used after you are experienced in all of the previous techniques, and should not be used instead of solid playing strategy. The opportunity to use misdirection is not great, but, remember, every strategic tool should be used when it can reduce the randomness of the game and give that little advantageous 'bump' that over time can enable your team to win.

The opportunity to use misdirection lies mainly with the defensive team, and is used to confuse the offensive team (mainly the Declarer) with what they analyze to be the dominos you are holding. The following chart shows some typical misdirection suggestions. These will not be conclusive, but will demonstrate how they may work.

Play	Analysis
5-0,4-1,3-2 Trump	If you have a 2nd or 3rd highest trump of any of these suits (5,4,3,2,1,0) and any of these 5 point counters, then a misdirection is to play the counter. Usually, a counter is played under duress, so this signals the Declarer that you are probably void in any other trumps and he may elect to not play the next highest to draw the higher trump, especially if you and Player 3 are the only trump players. This can leave you with a high trump for ambush purposes.
Trumps are in: Follow a non-trump high lead with a low domino of that suit instead of your double.	If you are in position to do so (especially last to play), then this play may throw off the lead player into thinking the double has already come in and he missed it, and he may come back with another play in that same suit, thinking it will walk.
10 point counters	Normally, most defensive players instinctively hold the highest counters, the 5-5 and 6-4 to the bitter end. However, what is the offensive team's bid? Can a 6-point trick set them? What if you as a defensive player, hold a 10 counter and one or two 5 counters? If so, at the first opportunity to follow a lead suit with a counter, play the 10-point counter. This indicates to the offensive players that you are void in trumps and that is your only counter. Hold your 5 counter(s) for a lead your defensive partner owns.
Declarer's opening play (offensive team misdirection)	From the previous section on 'when to play count', an opening play by the Declarer of a low lead can signal Player 2 to throw count if able so to not miss the only perceived opportunity to set the offensive team. With this knowledge, a Declarer, in certain situations, may elect to play a low lead to draw out the count from Player 2, realizing he has a 50-50 chance to gain it (Player 3 vs Player 4). This may only work if the offensive team has a low bid.
Declarer's opening play (offensive team misdirection)	Also from the previous section on 'when to play count', an opening play by the Declarer of a low trump can signal that he is trying to get out of the lead early in the hand so as to dump a dangerous off. If you, the Declarer have a complete suit of trumps, but a 5 or 10 counter off, then you could play your lowest trump domino. Player 2, faced with the only opportunity to set your team, may throw any count he may have. Hopefully, this count will be the one your off play might draw.

Figure 19 Misdirection Plays Table

Advanced Tips

The following section focuses on miscellaneous tips that can give the reader strategic advantages during the course of a game. They are:

- Bidding
- Plays
- Working your trumps
- Indicating (legal)

Bidding

Careful observation of how the opposing players (and your partner also) bid during the course of the game can provide some strategic advantages. Pay attention to the following:

Is an opposing player passing more often than normal?

> If this happens, it may mean he is a conservative player - someone that is not risking making bid with the help of his partner. This tendency can be used to your advantage if that player is bidding after you (on your left). If so and if Bidders 1 and 2 pass and you are Bidder 3, you may want to bid 31 on a bid you would normally take cheap so as to intimidate him into not bidding (remember the advantage goes to the bid-winning team). Or, conversely, you might test him by bidding 30 and see if he passes a few times, depending upon him to be cautious about bidding 31.

Does one of your opposing players avoid bidding between 31 and 42 (a mark), and what type of hand does he play on a 1 mark bid?

> Some players like drama in the game and enjoy declaring 'a mark' as bid. Do they have a near lay-down hand or do they frequently go set? If you do not have a good enough hand for a 2 mark bid, then you cannot overbid him and must settle for playing the strongest defensive round you can. Good, steady, players analyze their hand thoroughly and mentally compute how much they can lose, and thus may bid anywhere from 30 to 36 (a 36 bid means you gamble you will lose a 5 counter and the trick and still win the hand).

Does an opposing player following you consistently up your bid by one point?

> If this is happening, it shows that this player knows that the bid-winning team has the advantage and is very reluctant to allow the bid right to be lost. When he bids this way does he win the hand? If he does not consistently (i.e. 50-50), then it is good strategy to take advantage of his tendency and up the ante by making *your* bid a point or so higher. This may make him bid high on an average hand, and, consequently be settable.

Does any opposing player consistently make a high bid?

If this happens, this means that this player is an experienced player and knows how to judge his hand. If, during the bidding round he bids a high bid ahead of you, then if you have any playable hand at all, then overbid him as you will probably lose the hand anyway, and with the bid, you at least have a chance to make it. Remember, you do have a partner and together you have a greater chance to make your bid. Also, a player with a strong hand that bids high and does not get the bid – *may not have a setting hand when he is on defense*.

Why (and when to) bid a mark?

Since winning the hand gives the winning team a mark, why would a player bid a mark instead of say, a high bid? Strategically, bidding a mark is a psychological play – i.e. it raises the risk bar to the following bidders. Of course, if a player has a lay-down hand, then he would bid a mark so as to be sure to gain the bid. Another player could only up it by bidding two marks. But what if you have a strong trump hand? Many would bid a mark in this situation because bidding a mark appeals to their aggressive nature, adds excitement, or adds a little 'star' persona. However, many of these type players have gone set by one trick they didn't account for. To summarize; if you have a lay-down hand bid one or two marks, if you have a strong trump hand, bid 36. This way, in a worse case, you can lose a 5 counter trick and still win the hand. If you have a good enough hand that you feel that you can catch all of the counters, but still could lose a trick, and you don't want to lose the bid, then bid 40 or 41! When to bid 2 marks? If you have a lay-down hand and you need two marks to win the game, you should make a 2 mark bid. Of course, make sure that you don't lose the game if you lose the hand and those 2 marks go to your opponents!

When to up your partner's bid

Normally, upping your partners bid is not a good practice. However, the following reasons may apply:

- Your partner has consistently missed making his bid, and you have a strong enough hand to justify it. Do this, however, only if your partner's bid is low.
- Your partner is Bidder 1 and has opened bidding low, Bidder 2 has passed, and Bidder 4 has consistently bid aggressively.
- You have a lay-down or near lay-down hand.
- If you have the option for a Nello bid (you are Bidder 4) and Bidders 1 or 3 have bid. In this case it is good odds that Bidder 1 or 3 that have bid has a hand with a good spread of trumps and the remaining one has a mixed hand. These are good hands for taking tricks – which is what you want to happen in Nello.

It is evident from the above questions that bidding patterns are an important part of playing strategy if you know how to read them. What this means, in a game with evenly matched players, just a slight advantage may be all that is needed. That advantage may just lie in the bidding phase of the game.

Plays

The following chart lists some plays to watch for and the reason for them. When they appear, analyze your hand and respond accordingly. These plays are assumed to be made by experienced players so that they can be somewhat predictable. If you have a beginner or a player that is weird, then all bets are off. (Player 1 is the bid-winner):

Play	Analysis
Player 1 names trump but leads out with a non-trump (includes small-end lead option)	Player 1 holds a bothersome off that he feels he must get out of his hand and the best time to do this is on the first play when the maximum dominos are in play.
Player 1 leads with a trump-6 instead of the double	Player 1 does not have the double but has enough trumps so that after an opposing player captures the first trick, he can trump back in and capture the remaining tricks. If you have count and no trump, and you are Player 2, then you might consider playing the count now in hopes of your partner having the double (it is 50-50 at this point). If you don't and the bid-winner gets by this first round, he may be in a position to run the rest.
Player 1 leads with a low trump	Player 1 has perhaps the 2 highest trumps, but another 2 that are the lower. So like the no double lead above, he needs to draw in the mid-count trumps at the time of least damage. He can also hope his partner has some of them. If the partner does, he should capture with his highest trump. Of course he might also have had the bid dropped on him and that may be his best trump!
A count domino of led suit is played by defensive player	Generally, this indicates that this is the only domino of that lead suit in his hand. Do not repeat this lead if this happens as the next round he may trump in!
A double of another suit is played on a lead by any other player	Since the double is the most valuable domino in a suit, this would indicate this players 'offs' are doubles (he might have been bidding on a doubles trump hand). Knowing this, be careful of any non-double leads you may subsequently play as he could catch them.
Player 2 or 4 captures a trump lead. Leads out in a new lead with 6-6 or 4-4 (if not trump)	These are the defensive team players and they are fishing for the 6-4 to set the offensive team. The one playing these leads will not have the 6-4 so if you do not possess it, you can assume it is held by the other two players. If the defensive partner answers this lead with another 6 or 4 suit domino, then it can be assumed that your partner holds it.

Player 3 captures a trump lead. Leads out with a 0-0,1-1,2-2,3-3 (if not trump)	Player 3 is attempting to draw out a 5 counter so as to help make his team's bid.
Player 3 captures a trump lead. Leads out with a 6-6 or 4-4 (if not trump)	Same as above but now attempting to draw out a 10 counter from the defensive team.
Player 1 leads a non-trump double after 2 highest trump leads	Player 1 may be missing the 3rd and-or 4th highest trump and is trying to draw as much count as possible, and-or letting his partner gain the lead.
A partner player plays an off instead of count on his partner's first lead	Bad news from Player 1's viewpoint! This means his partner is void in counters. However, this is an important piece of information – he just has to adjust (if possible).

Figure 20 Plays Analyses Table

Working Your Trumps

Many teams' winning hands are lost by the Declarer misplaying his trumps. This section will provide some guidelines for the best way to utilize different trump inventories and combinations:

Trump Inventory	Analysis
Hand has all 7 trumps	Lay-down hand
Hand has 6 trumps but not the double	Player 1 can lead any trump (doesn't matter which) on the first play to draw out the double and get it out of the way with the least damage. Of course if Player 2 plays the double and Player 4 has big count, be prepared to lose at least 11 points. You need to have a bid where you can lose this amount and hope your one off can walk.
Hand has 5 trumps but not the double and T-6 (Trump-6)	This hand, although risky, can be won as long as your bid isn't higher than say, 31. Your hope is that your partner has at least one of the high trumps. Lead any of your trumps on the first play and see if your partner can help. If one defensive player has both trumps you will probably go set, if they are split between the two, then you can pull it off.
Hand has 2 high trumps	This trump inventory works only if the remaining trumps are evenly distributed among the other players. If the first trump play is answered by only one defensive player, then you are probably in deep doo-doo. If it is your partner only following suit, then 'happy days' are here again.
Hand has 2 high trumps and a low trump	Play the double on the first play and see how the remaining trumps are distributed. If all the other players follow trump lead, then play the second highest to draw in the remaining trump. (Player 1 has 3 trumps + 3 trumps on first round = 6). If your partner does not play trump on first round, then play the low trump on the second

[82]

	round and hope that Player 4 has the extra trump (Player 2 may not play count as he does not know where the other trump is). If Player 2 over-trumps you then Player 4 will dump count if he has it. If you still are in the lead, round 3 should be led with your doubles or other high leads so as to get as much count as possible before your last trump trick is caught by the higher defensive trump still out. Setting situation with this hand is that a defensive player has ALL of the remaining trumps.
Hand has double trump and a low trump	Generally, a pretty risky hand and would be the result of a forced bid. Play the low trump first so as to see the trump distribution and avoid the worst damage. Hopefully your partner can catch the trick and run a few leads to help. If it is end-game and you are the 4th player in a subsequent lead where count falls, then use the last trump.
Hand has the T-5, T-4, T-3 and T-2 (other than 5 trump)	This can be a good hand if you have one of the 10 counters and your bid is no more than 30 or 31 as you could lose 2 or more tricks. Lead out with any one of your trumps and see what the distribution is and who catches it. If the only trump is played by a defensive player, then you are likely set unless your partner has the other 10 spot and your offs are not hit by the defensive lead-back.
Hand has the 5-5, 4-4, 3-3 and 2-2 on a 'doubles' trump call	Lead out any double so as to pull in the 6-6. Here, you hope that the other defensive player is not void in doubles and does not have high count on the first round. If you get past round one, then you need to have your offs eliminated on the lead-back so as to regain the lead.
Hand has the 4-4, 3-3, 2-2, 1-1 and 0-0 on a 'doubles' trump call	This is a great hand if your partner has the 5-5. If he doesn't and the two other trumps are split between the defensive players, then your bid cannot be over 31 as you will lose at least 11 points (5-5 +trick).

Figure 21 Trumps Plays Analyses Table

Indicating

The last strategic tactic we will cover is what is called 'indicating'. Indicating is the practice of communicating to your partner key dominos you may hold so that on his next lead he can lead out a domino that can work with your 'indicated' one. As you may recall, in the section on protocols, it is illegal or at least unethical to 'signal' your partner with body movements, code words, etc. However, it is accepted in recreational play that one can signal by what domino is played. Indicating of any type is not allowed in tournament play.

There is considerable controversy about indicating – what it is, how valuable it is, and whether it is legal to use and when.

I would rather use good analysis as outlined in this chapter to determine the domino to be played, instead of depending upon a faulty system to let a partner know what a player holds – a method that does not necessarily mean that the best team or players win the game. However, if you think that indicating is your cup of tea, then the following shows you how to play it.

Indicating uses the idea of –
- bidding values to show the numbers of doubles one might have at bidding time, or,
- by the value of the high end of the off domino played, transmitting what doubles may be in a player's hand during play.

Indicating at Bid Time

Partners are not allowed to talk across the table about the dominos they're holding (or how they should be played). However, a player may signal to his partner that he has three or more doubles (dominos with the same number of dots on each end) by bidding 30, provided he is the first bidder, or all previous players passed (and his partner has not bid yet).

Once a partner has passed (and no preceding player has bid), the other partner can bid 30 without necessarily holding any doubles. In any case, partners trying to make a bid usually should indicate their double(s) when able, even if fewer than three are held.

Indicating During Play

Indicating has limited use since not only your partner can read the indication, but also the *opposition* team members. In addition, not only can a domino indicate a lead-back play, but it can also miss-indicate if there is no domino choice. A good example would be Player 1 plays a lead where his partner does not need to follow and must play a 3-1 off (other dominos are counters or trump). If Player 1 reads the 3-1 as indicating that Player 2 is holding the 3-3, then he would lead back with the 3-2. However, Player 2 or 4 may have the 3-3 and consequently catches the trick and count.

One may not want to bid 30 unless he can "indicate" at least one of his doubles to his partner. This is done by playing a domino with the high end equal to one end of a held double when the player cannot follow suit in a trick. If that is not possible, the double can be played if the next highest domino is also held, e.g., the double-three indicates the player has the next highest three 6-3. If more than one double can be indicated, indicate the highest double(s) first.

CONCLUSION

As mentioned at the beginning of this chapter, you will find, when you have played 42 for a time, the pace of the game goes too fast to calculate moves from the previous strategies. However, by learning them and practicing with others or with a computer game, you can progress to the point where you can greatly reduce the normal **random factor** inherent in the dealt hands and make losing hands into winning ones!

New Terms covered:

Junk Hand – A hand that does not have any redeemable value for any style of 42 played

Helper Hand – A hand that has either missing trumps, count or few doubles or a combination of all three

Average Trump Hand – A hand with a few high trumps including the double, and several good leads (doubles or doubles plus next highest)

Strong Trump Hand – A hand with four high trumps, including the double and no more than one off

Tournament Play

*"Every tournament has its climax, its winning moment.
If you're not watchful, you will miss it and lose your best chance"*
- Peter Thomson, Australian golfer

Now that you have 'upped' your 42 skills, you might be wanting to play against others with this 'killer' knowledge.

There are two types of tournaments we will address – informal and formal. Informal tournaments are not necessarily governed by accepted formal rules, although there is nothing wrong with patterning them after the formal tournaments. But, the rules can simply be what the host determines. What we will discuss here are some suggestions for 42 parties.

Formal tournaments are a different situation. 42 started life as a recreational game at the friends and family level. However, as with many games, it has progressed to the point where we now have competitive tournaments for 42 bragging rights. If you feel like you have advanced to the point that you belong in a tournament, then the following can give you an idea what tournaments are like. Personally, I think one has to have a streak of masochism to be willing to subject oneself to being repeatedly crushed by a team that seems to read each other's mind, knows every trick in the book, and are not real gracious winners (but, in a friendly way). But…whatever.

On the other hand, formal tournaments can be a lot of fun and you can meet some great folks who also love 42. These tournaments are regularly held in different locations. For information on tournament locations check the bibliography section.

Informal Tournaments

The first item, if you decide to have a 42 party, is to make sure you have a number of guests that is divisible by four. This is not unlike a Dubs Bridge party except you can have any of the number 4, 8, 12, or so on. You should have a card table or equivalent for every four players. It is also a good idea to have scoring pads and pens and domino sets for all tables. Of course, don't forget the refreshments!

Having a scoreboard like a whiteboard to record the teams and their scores is also a nice touch. If you have more than two teams, then you can use an elimination system to determine an eventual winner. The following is a suggestion on how this could work with different numbers of teams (2 players):

- One table, two teams, four players – eat pretzels, swig some beer and play 42 as long as you want!
- Two tables, four teams, eight players – simple team-table rotation per the table as follows:
- Three or more tables with 12 or more teams -

If you are getting up to this number of attendees, then a more organized way to determine the winner(s) is needed. This would include:
1) Each team plays two games versus every other team in the tournament.
2) The two teams with the best records will play a '2 out of 3' match for 1st place.
3) The teams with the 3rd and 4th best records will play a '2 out of 3' match for 3rd place.

Using the guidelines above, you can set up a playing schedule for eight teams so that each team plays every other team as indicated. Other optional competition arrangements include 'single elimination' and 'double elimination'.

Formal Tournaments

Tournament play is usually a lot stricter than recreational 42, with few or no variations allowed and definite protocols that must be followed. Generally, it most closely matches the 'Basic 42' definition in this book. So if you live and breathe Nello, tournament play may not be for you.

Here is a sample formal tournament program.

First, there will be a schedule:

> 1 PM Registration
> 1:30 PM Round Robin begins
> 3:20 PM Round Robin complete
> 3:30 PM Tournament begins
> 5:30 PM Tournament complete

And, any requirements:

> Each player is requested to bring a set of dominoes to the tournament, if possible. No player will be allowed to play with his-her own dominoes.

The Round Robin is described:
- All 16 teams will be broken into 4 groups of 4 teams.
- Each group of 4 teams will play each other once (3 games total).
- The marks for each game will be added together, and the 2 teams with the highest total of marks will proceed to the single-elimination tournament.
- No more than 7 marks will be awarded in any one game.
- If a tie occurs for first place, all players will draw a single domino. Adding both sides of each domino, the team having the highest combined total will be the first place team.
- If a tie occurs for second place, a one-hand tie breaker will be played to determine who proceeds to the tournament round.

- When time is called to end the Round Robin, any games still in progress must complete their current hand and then stop the game.

The Tournament itself is defined:

The 8 teams from the Round Robin will enter a single-elimination tournament. During the first round, the top team from each round robin group will play the 2nd place team of another group. The winning team of the tournament will receive a cash prize of $100 and the 2nd place team will receive $50 (cash prize may be reduced if fewer than 16 teams enter the tournament).

Of course, with any tournament there have to be Rules:
1) To begin play, each player draws one domino with the highest draw (adding both sides of domino) winning the first shuffle. Ties to be redrawn by the tying players.
2) The "domino shaker" role rotates clock-wise, and the person the left of the shaker bids first.
3) Maximum initial bids of two marks high, with overbidding limited to one mark above the previous bid.
4) The first team to 7 marks or higher wins.
5) Each player is allowed 20 seconds to make a bid.
6) Dominoes must be set on table with back row of 4 dominoes & front row of 3 dominoes and may not be rearranged during play. If everyone agrees, dominoes may be held in hand instead.
7) "Low" bids are not allowed, unless the first 3 bidders all pass. The last bidder then has the option of going low. Doubles can be high, low, or a suit of their own.
8) "No trump" (Follow me) bids are allowed.
9) "Sevens," "Splash," and "Plunge" bids are NOT allowed.
10) Bids of two marks or more should be stacked.
11) A domino laid is a domino played.
12) Trump suit (or no trump) must be called BEFORE first domino is played; otherwise, the suit of first domino played will be trump suit.
13) Any attempt of "talking across the table" will result in loss of hand.
14) Renege (misplay) counts as a loss of the hand.
15) No player substitutions are allowed after the tournament has begun.

Here is a very detailed tournament rules sheet:

Tournament Rules
Game Play Rules:
Straight 42 for all tournaments
Forced Bid
Minimum Bid is 30
No Plunge, No Nello, No Sevens
Follow Me High

Other Tournament Rules:
Draw for first shake. High domino shakes the dominoes first.
No talking across the table during the play of each hand. Talking allowed after someone has played all his dominoes.
No signs or signals to be used. Doing so brings about disqualification.
Dominoes must be played on the table without "pointing" (the manner in which you play your domino must not appear to be communicating your hand to your partner).
Dominoes will be placed on the table in a 4-3 or 3-4 configuration. Once set, they may not be moved except to play a domino in turn. Dominoes are set at the time of your bid.
Dominoes will be stacked on all 1-mark or greater bids. The most recent two tricks will be visible during the stacking process.
The touch rule is in effect. If you touch a domino on your turn, you are required to play it.
You may turn over dominoes and declare victory ("I have the rest") or a lay-down. The same applies to having the high trump that will set the opponent. Your must prove your case and your opponent must agree before moving on to the next hand. Loss of hand will result if you do this in error.
Loss of hand results from the following:
Playing out of turn.
Failure to follow suit when you could have followed suit.
Exposing a domino that will not play when it is your turn to play.
Exposing any domino when it is not your turn.
Bumping the table or causing dominoes to fall over and be exposed.
Mistaken announcement of victory-lay-down of dominoes or in claiming a set where dominoes are exposed (see rule above).
Picking up more than 7 dominoes and looking at them before a hand is played.
Failure to use the 3-4 or 4-3 domino setup at the start of the hand.
Visitors may watch the games, but they may not move around during the hand, nor be a distraction to the game.
First team to get 7 marks wins. Since there is a time limit, if neither team has 7 marks when the game-over timer ends the game, the hand is completed and the team with the most marks wins. If the score is tied, one additional hand is played for a winner.
If a team fails to be in place for a game five minutes after the starting timer, then the game is forfeited by the team with the missing member.
At the conclusion of the game, one player from each team will initial or sign the opponents score sheet.
Players may begin play of their next game before the official start time if all four players are ready to play (excluding the first game, which will start at the conclusion of the announcements). Games will run 25 minutes.
Tie breakers for advancing from the round robin to the championship bracket: Top two teams advance. If there is a tie for either position, the following rules will determine the winner. If the tie is a two-way tie, the winner is determined by the winner of their game in the round robin. If the tie is a three-way tie, the winners will be chosen by total marks scored by each team during the round robin. Any ties in number of marks will be broken by the winner of the round robin game between those who tied. If 3 teams tied in both wins and marks, then high draw of the dominoes will determine who advances.

Figure 22 Sample Tournament Program

Here's a simple, or what might be called a 'quick and dirty' tournament program:

- Tournament is double elimination.
- Play to seven marks.
- Entry fee is $5 per person. First place wins 70%, second wins 20%, and the consolation winner receives 10%.
- Rules: No 7's, Minimum bid is 30, Plunge (requires 4 doubles) is for 3 marks, Splash (requires 3 doubles) is for 2 marks, Force Nello, Maximum opening bid is 2-marks, Maximum raise is 2 marks, Stack dominoes on 2-mark or more hands, Follow Me doubles can be high or a suit of their own, Nello doubles can be high, low, or a suit of their own.

Here's another tournament program that has what we could call a 'Dirty Harry' attitude!

- Normal tournament rules* apply.
- NO NELLO, NO FORCED BID! If the bid comes all the way around to the dealer, he can bid or re-shake.
- No Two Mark Bids. The highest leading bid is one mark and they can be bumped one mark at a time from there.
- On multiple mark hands, dominoes can be single or double stacked (or not stacked at all) - bidder's choice.
- No sevens, splash, plunge, "Partner, I need a little help!" or any other funny business! Just straight 42!
- Each team plays 2 games vs. every other team in the tournament. The two teams with the best records will play a "2 out of 3" match for 1st place.
- The teams with the 3rd and 4th best records will play a "2 out of 3" match for 3rd place.
- There will be no substituting if a player becomes unable to play.
- Prize amounts will be determined at the time of the tournament.

You don't like the rules? Make my day!

As we can see from these sample programs, tournament rules and conditions can vary somewhat. And, that is the prerogative of the tournament hosts. However, the common requirements we see running through them all are; match prerequisites, protocols, penalties, variations rulings, and entry fees and prizes.

One of the more complex aspects of a tournament, whether informal or formal, is how to determine the overall winning team. This is done through a two-step process where teams play in a round-robin phase, and then proceed to a single or double elimination step. Or, there may be just a single and-or double elimination step – the number of teams and the tournament hosts make this determination.

How do these processes work? The goal is for every team to play every other team or the team that has beaten other teams, and, if in case of a loss, a chance to overcome it (double elimination). It is like a sports competition where there is double elimination, the field is essentially halved each round until the final two teams meet.

Layout and other suggestions:

1) The playing area should be a pleasant room with no distracting movements or noises, and be of a comfortable temperature.
2) The playing tables and chairs should be the same for all players. The playing tables should be sturdy enough so that an accidental nudge from a player's knee doesn't produce four 'lay-up' hands.
3) There should be a separate lounge area for those not currently playing so that those playing are not distracted.

Elimination Trees

The following player elimination trees are often used:

Single elimination tournament with contestants in powers of two.

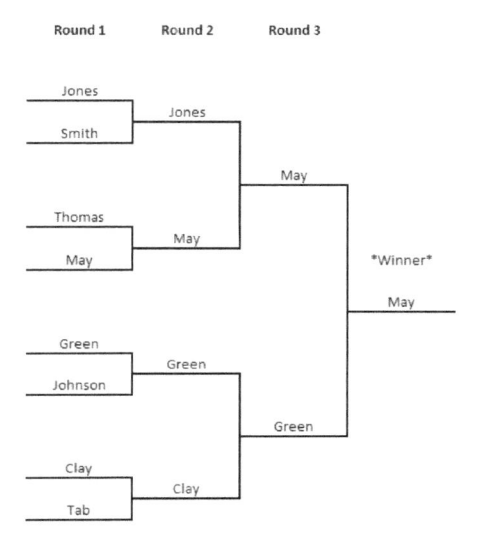

Single elimination tournament with byes. This shows that Jones, May, and Thomas do not play in Round 1.

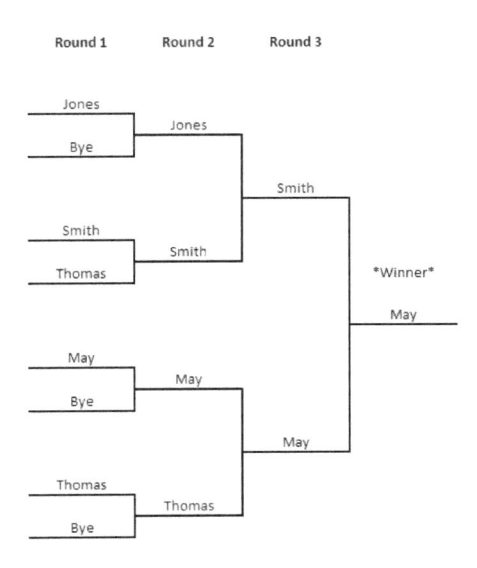

Double Elimination

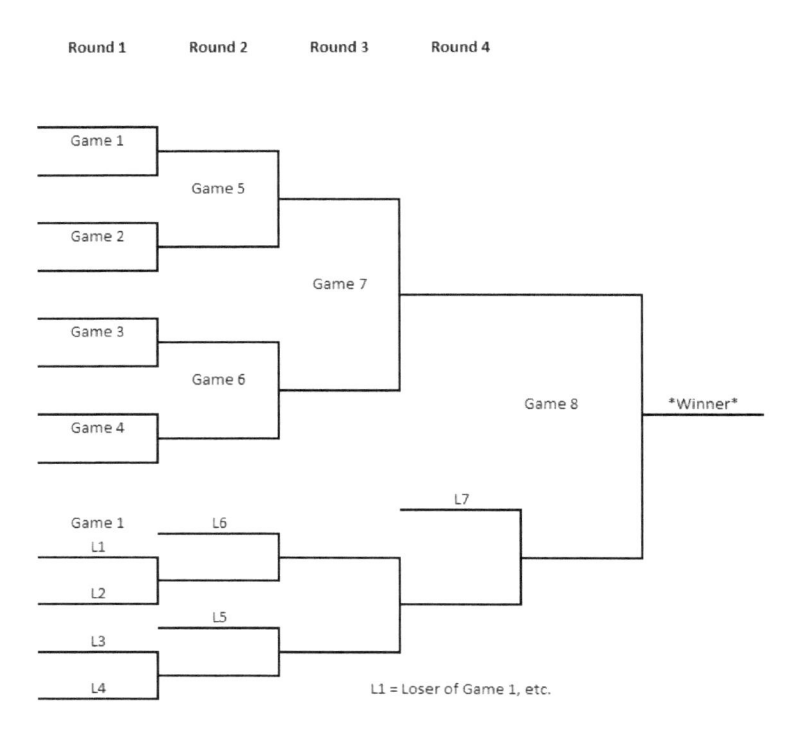

```
Round 1      Round 2      Round 3      Round 4

Game 1
         Game 5
Game 2
                     Game 7
Game 3
         Game 6
Game 4
                                  Game 8    *Winner*

                              L7
Game 1   L6
  L1
  L2
         L5
  L3
  L4                 L1 = Loser of Game 1, etc.
```

New Terms covered:

Tournament – A competitive setting for serious 42 players

Trees - The 'map' of the competing teams schedule

Informal Tournament – A tournament played by family or friends (usually food and beer involved)
Formal Tournament – A tournament sponsored by a club or organization, usually with prizes or prize money (and bragging rights)
Round – Play by the teams matched up – each subsequent round being half of the teams from the previous round

Forms for Your Use

"What we imagine is order is merely the prevailing form of chaos."
- Kerry Thornley (from the introduction to Principia Discordia, 5th edition, by Malaclypse)

Please feel free to copy and use any of the following forms for your personal use (but not commercially).

Game Rules Form

42 Game Rules

Game Type	Basic ☐	Variations ☐
Scoring	Marks ☐	Points ☐
Forced Bid Required	Yes ☐	No ☐
Small End Lead Allowed	Yes ☐	No ☐
Nello	Yes ☐	No ☐
Any Player Call	Yes ☐	No ☐
Dealer Only – Any Bid	Yes ☐	No ☐
Dealer Only – 30 Bid only	Yes ☐	No ☐
Plunge	Yes ☐	No ☐
Splash	Yes ☐	No ☐
Sevens	Yes ☐	No ☐
Other:		

Figure 23 Game Rules Form

Scorecard 1 – Marks

42 Scorecard

Table Number _____

Team 1	Team 2
_____ _____	_____ _____
—	—

| Game 1 |
| Game 2 |
| Game 3 |
| Game 4 |
| Game 5 |
| Game 6 |
| Game 7 |

Figure 24 Score Card Form - Marks

Scorecard 2 – Points

42 Scorecard

Table Number _____

Team 1	Team 2
_____ _____ —	_____ _____ —

Game 1

Points _____	Points _____

Game 2

+ Points _____ = _____	+ Points _____ = _____

Game 3

+ Points _____ = _____	+ Points _____ = _____

Game 4

+ Points _____ = _____	+ Points _____ = _____

Game 5

+ Points _____ = _____	+ Points _____ = _____

Game 6

+ Points _____ = _____	+ Points _____ = _____

Game 7

+ Points _____ = _____	+ Points _____ = _____

Team Total

_____	_____

Figure 25 Score Card Form – Points

Miscellaneous Facts and Information

"Facts are stubborn things, but statistics are more pliable"
Mark Twain, American Humorist

Counts and Odds Statistics

What follows are some statistics about the game of 42, the dominos, hands, and plays that you might find interesting.

- The odds of drawing a specific hand from the bone-yard of 28 dominos are 1 in 5,967,561,600.
- The odds of drawing all seven dominoes of a suit from the bone-yard at the beginning of a game is 1 in 1,184,040.
- If you hold 4 trumps, the odds of your partner holding the other three are 1 in 9.
- If you hold 4 trumps, the odds of your two opponents holding the other three are 8 in 9.
- If you hold 4 trumps, the odds of one each being held by the other players are 1 in 9.
- If you hold 3 trumps, the odds of your partner holding the other four are 1 in 12.
- If you hold 3 trumps, the odds of your two opponents holding the other four are 7 in 12.
- The odds of having a strong trump hand with the three highest trumps, three doubles, and an off is 1 in 37.
- There are a total of 37 strong trump hands (above).
- The odds of a lay-down Sevens hand (ex: 6-1, 5-2, 4-3, 6-2, 5-3, 4-4, 6-3) is……shoot! You figure this one out!
- There are a total of 168 dots (pips) on the 28 dominos in a set of double-six dominos.
- There are 791 lay-down hand combinations in Basic 42.

Bidding Chart

The following chart lists the bid limits with each variation of 42 and the accompanying bidding rules.

Variation	Min Bid	Max Bid Possible	Explanation
Basic 42	30	5 marks	Maximum opening bid is 2 marks, each following Bidder (3) may up bid by 1 mark each.
Sevens	42	5 marks	Same as above.
Nello	42	5 marks	Same as above.
Plunge	4 marks	7 marks	Must open a Plunge hand with a bid of 4 marks. Following bidders may up each bid by a mark each.
Splash	3 marks	6 marks	Must open a Splash hand with a bid of 3 marks. Following bidders may up each bid a mark each.

Figure 26 Bidding Chart

Frequently Asked Questions

"No question is ever settled until it is settled right."
- Author and Poet Ella Wheeler Wilcox

If you have specific questions about the game of 42, you will hopefully find them in the following answers:

Q: Can any number other than four play 42?
  A: No, the game only works with two teams of two players each. Moon is a similar game for three players.

Q: What are the dots on the dominos called?
  A: The dots on dominos are called pips.

Q: How many dominos does each player get?
  A: Each player gets seven dominos (28 dominos in set - 4 players).

Q: Can any suit be trumps, and how do I tell the difference between them and the other dominoes?
  A: When declared, trumps become the highest of all the possible domino suits. The non-trump end of a trump domino designates its ranking in the trump suit and has no relationship whatsoever with non-trump dominos.

Q: Can you call doubles as your trump?
  A: Yes. Trumps would be the 6-6 through 0-0 dominos. The 6-6 is the highest trump.

Q: Can I call Nello anytime I win the bid?
  A: Normally not, unless that variation is called. If the Nello variation is allowed, the default is that only the last bidder may call it if he has the bid forced upon him. Another variation is that the last bidder may call it even if others have bid. And the last variation is that any player may call Nello at any time.

Q: Must a player play a domino with the led suit on one end, if it has the trump suit on the other end?
  A: No. Trumps are a suit of their own. A domino with a led suit on one end and the trump suit on the other belongs to the trump suit. The opposite end from the trump end merely sets the points value of that particular trump.

Q: If trumps are called, do they have to be led or can you lead out a non-trump?
  A: No, trumps do not have to be led, but you must always call trumps before the play.

Q: If Doubles are a suit of their own, and a double cannot be played, does a domino with one end the same suit as the double have to be played?
  A: No. A player can play any domino he chooses.

Q: When playing Sevens, if the declarer's partner takes the lead on a trick does he keep the lead or does it revert back to the declarer?
  A: When the declarer's partner wins a trick, the partner leads the next domino (whoever wins a trick always leads the next domino).

Q: What is more important in 42, luck or skill?

A: While the luck of the draw can at times be more beneficial (like a lay-down hand), over time skill and strategy (as covered in this book) will be more important.

Q: When you are playing in a tournament, what is a 'bye'?

A: A 'bye' means that you can advance to the next round without playing an opponent. This happens when there are an odd number of players in a competition.

Q: Can multiple marks be bid in a hand, and if so, can the bid be the number of marks needed to win the game?

A: The first bid in marks can be a maximum of one or two marks for Basic 42. Subsequent bidders may up the bid by one mark each. See the Bid table on page **99.**

Q: Are there any situations where a person can bid less than 30 points?

A: Basic 42 has a minimum bid of 30. There are variations for minimum bids of more than 30 but none for less.

Q: What is meant by the terms "follow me high" or "follow me low"?

A: These are the 'follow me' variations with the treatment of the double during play. Follow me low means that the play is follow me and doubles are the lowest of the suits – follow me high means that doubles are the highest in the suits.

Q: If you wanted to score by points instead of marks, how would the points count in a played hand when the bidder does not make his bid? Does the opposing team get the amount bid plus tricks and count?

A: See scoring section on page 20.

Q: Is 'indicating' acceptable in tournament play?

A: Most tournaments would not allow any system to 'indicate' what one player may hold to his partner. For recreational play, the players can use any rules that they agree upon.

Q: Where would you find information on tournaments?

A: See Bibliography.

Q: How would a person find out how best to organize and run a friends and family tournament?

A: See the Tournaments chapter for a 42 party organization.

Glossary

"Knowledge is power"
- Sir Francis Bacon

42 (Texas 42): A domino game for four people (partnered pairs), women and men, similar to the card game Bridge (but less complicated), with bidding and trumps; played by young and old for fun and-or competition

Basic 42: Plain 42 with traditional rules and limited game variations (subject to individual and regional interpretation). Formal competition rules vary, but they normally specify exclusions.

Bid: The declaration of the number of points (tricks plus count) that a player thinks he and his partner can win in a hand. Bids vary from 30 to 41, one mark (42), to multiple marks.

Boneyard: The pile of shuffled dominos in the center of the table is euphemistically referred to as the 'bone-yard'.

Call in: Lead a suit, especially trumps, to bring a particular domino out into play that could later jeopardize making your bid or your ability to set the opponents.

Come: When you're in the lead, and you need your partner to take the lead so you can unload your 'off' domino(s), you 'come' to your partner, i.e., lead a domino that you think he can take and win the trick.

Count: Count is the five dominos with face values divisible by 5, such as 3-2, 4-1, 5-0, 5-5 and 6-4. Each count domino is worth its face value in points.

Dominos: The rectangular tiles used to play 42 and other domino games. A set of double-six dominos has 28 tiles.

Double: A double has the same number of pips on each end. There are seven doubles in a set of double-six dominos, the 6-6, 5-5, 4-4, 3-3, 2-2, 1-1, and 0-0. The double is the highest rank in its suit.

Draw: After the dominos are shuffled to begin a new hand, each player picks (draws) seven dominos before beginning play. (The shuffler draws last.)

Dropped Bid: In the bidding process, when the last bidder (the shuffler) has to take the bid because the other three players passed, he has the bid "dropped" on him.

False indicator: When a partner plays an off domino that doesn't indicate he's holding the high domino in that suit, his domino is a "false indicator."

Follow me: A variation to Basic 42. When a player gets the bid and doesn't want to call a trump suit (no trumps), he can say "follow me." This means the highest domino played takes each trick.

Hand: A hand is the seven tricks played following each shuffle in a game. Also refers to the seven dominos held by a player.

House rules: These are the established playing rules defined by the hosting individual(s) or game director for tournaments.

Acceptable variations and penalties for indiscretions are spelled out.

Indicate: A method of letting a partner know when a lead following player that he has a high domino of a suit so the partner can come to him to make bid.

Lay down: This is a hand that cannot be set. The Declarer says he has a 'lay down' hand and reveals his dominos to show that he would take all the tricks if play continued.

Lead: The first domino played in a trick. It defines the suit to be followed, be it trump or otherwise.

Low (Nel-o): See Nello below.

Mark: The score pad annotation when a bid is made (or set). Each hand won or lost is a mark unless multiple marks were bid. Seven marks by either team win the game.

Nello: A 42 variation whereby only the Declarer and the opposing team members play (3). The Declarer's partner lays his dominos down during the course of the hand.

Offs: Dominos that are not part of your trump suit or to any of your high lead suits. Many assume that an off has no value. That is not true, as an off that can walk could capture as much as 30 points!

Opening: The first lead in the first trick of a hand. The Declarer leads the first domino and calls trumps or other play at this time.

Overtrump: When a player plays a trump in lieu of another lead, and a subsequent player plays a higher trump, this is an 'overtrump'.

Partner: The person sitting opposite you at the playing table.

Pass: A player may pass during bidding if he does not want to bid. Some players 'knock' on the table to indicate they pass.

Pip: Pips are the dots on each face of a domino that defines its suit and value.

Points: There are 42 possible points in a hand: seven tricks (each trick is a point) plus the five count dominos totaling 35 points. Each hand is scored as a mark unless multiple marks were bid.

Protocol: The rules and etiquettes established for the game.

Renege: Not following suit when a domino is led, e.g., a two is led, you have a two, but you play something else. Reneging is cause for a team to lose the round.

Round: See 'trick'.

Rules: Acceptable play agreed on before play begins. For recreational play, all players may agree on any standard defined rules and-or variations. For tournament play the rules will be published for all players.

Score: The team who scores seven marks first wins the game. Marks are annotated on paper by spelling "ALL" (each letter segment is a mark). There is a variation of scoring by points. (see page

Set: When the winning bid team does not make their bid, they are set, and the opposing team gets the mark or marks, depending upon the bid.

Shake: Same as Shuffle.

Shuffle:	Mixing up all 28 dominos by mixing them face down on the playing surface.
Stack:	When the high bid is one or more marks, the dominos won in each trick are stacked face-up so only the last two tricks are shown.
Straight off:	A straight off is an off domino whose pips on either end match none of the other suits in your hand.
Suit:	A suit is the seven dominos with the same number of pips on one end, e.g., the five suit is the 5-5, 5-6, 5-4, 5-3, 5-2, 5-1 and 5-0.
Take the trick:	When you 'take' a trick, you win the trick by having the highest domino played.
Throw off:	Get rid of or unload an undesirable domino when you do not have to follow suit in a trick.
Trick:	The domino led and the three subsequent dominos played constitute a trick. There are seven tricks in a normal hand. Each trick taken is worth one point.
Trump:	The domino suit named by the winning bidder (Declarer) at the start of a hand. It always outranks the other six suits. The double is the highest domino of the trump (Basic 42).
Trump set:	What happens when you make a bid with either too few trumps, or not enough high count ones. If your opponents have more trumps than your team, you can become 'trump set'.
Unload:	Same as 'throw off', above.
Variations:	Different or optional rules agreed on before beginning a game, e.g., Nello, Plunge, Sevens, Splash, Small-end Lead, etc.
Walker:	A 'walker' is a domino lead that no other player can follow. For example, if you lead the 3-0, and all the other 3's have been played, then the 3-0 is a walker.

Bibliography

"Knowledge is of two kinds. We know a subject ourselves, or we know where we can find information on it"
Samuel Johnson

Historical Sources
Kathleen E. and Clifton R. St. Clair, eds., *Little Towns of Texas* (Jacksonville, Texas: Jayroe Graphic Arts, 1982).

Suppliers and Providers

Puremco Manufacturing Company, the only company in the United States that still makes dominoes, is in Waco, Texas. Their URL is www.dominoes.com

Tournaments

The official Texas state championship 42 tournament is held each March in Hallettsville, Texas. Check it online here: www.hallettsville.com/pages/dominos.html (or go to www.hallettsville.com and check their calendar of events)

The National 42 Players Association Rankings is www.n42pa.com
You can see the serious players' rankings and a lot of other great information

Killer 42 Website

You can visit my website www.killer42.com for purchase of this book plus a lot more things domino like dominoes and playing tables, tournaments, and 42 references.

Index

7

7 marks, 27, 88, 89, 90, 100

A

Advanced Tips, 79
ALL, 20, 26, 83, 96, 104
Analyzing a Drawn hand, 65
Analyzing a Drawn Hand, 63
Analyzing Plays in a Trick, 67
Analyzing the End-Game, 69
Average Trump Hand, 38, 41, 85

B

Basic 42, 29, 88
Bibliography, 102, 106
bid and match method, 18
Bidding, 18, 29, 32, 37, 40, 51, 79, 99, 100
bidding phase, 14, 81
Bumgarner, 12

C

Communication, 17
contracts, 29, 32
count, 14, 20, 23, 26, 27, 31, 34, 38, 39, 41, 42, 45, 46, 47, 48, 50, 51, 52, 53, 55, 56, 57, 62, 64, 67, 68, 69, 70, 73, 74, 75, 76, 78, 81, 82, 83, 84, 85, 102, 103, 104, 105
counter, 22, 25, 27, 31, 37, 39, 41, 42, 43, 45, 46, 48, 49, 50, 51, 52, 53, 55, 56, 64, 65, 66, 67, 68, 70, 71, 72, 73, 76, 77, 78, 79, 80, 82
Counters, 15, 16, 32, 52, 53, 64, 69, 70, 71
Counts and Odds Statistics, 99

D

Declarer, 14, 26, 27, 30, 31, 33, 34, 45, 46, 47, 48, 49, 50, 56, 62, 67, 72, 73, 74, 76, 77, 78, 82, 104, 105
Direction of Play, 21

double elimination, 88, 91, 92
Double Elimination, 94
Doubles Catch Doubles, 44
doubles high, 33
Doubles High, 33, 43
doubles low, 33
Doubles Low, 33, 43
Doubles Option Rankings, 33
doubles take the trick, 33
dropped bid, 29

E

Elimination Trees, 93

F

Flow of play, 21
Follow Me, 29, 30, 31, 32, 42, 89, 91
forced, 29
formal, 10, 32, 87, 88, 91
Formal Tournaments, 88
Forms for Your Use, 95
Frequently Asked Questions, 101

G

Game Rules Form, 95
Garner, 11, 12, 13
Glossary, 103

H

hand', 14
Handling of the dominoes, 17
Hands void of trumps, 51
Helper Hand, 38, 85
Hiding Trumps, 51

I

Indicating, 79, 83, 84, 103
Informal tournaments, 87
Informal Tournaments, 87

[107]

J

Junk Hand, 38, 41, 85

L

Lay down' Hand, 17
Lead following practices, 51
Lead Following Practices, 51
leads, 22, 23, 30, 31, 34, 41, 42, 46, 47, 48, 49, 50, 51, 52, 53, 56, 59, 62, 64, 65, 66, 67, 68, 70, 72, 73, 74, 75, 76, 81, 82, 83, 85, 101, 104
Leads, 53, 64, 74, 81, 82
Likely Lead Inventory, 69, 71
Loss of hand, 90

M

mark, 17, 18, 19, 20, 21, 26, 27, 30, 32, 34, 35, 38, 42, 44, 51, 63, 73, 79, 80, 89, 90, 91, 100, 102, 103, 104
marks, 18, 27, 30, 32, 34, 80, 88, 89, 90, 91, 100, 102, 103, 104, 105
Mineral Wells, 12, 13
Miscellaneous Facts and Information, 99
Misdirection, 77, 78
Misplaying, 17

N

Nello, 29, 32, 33, 34, 35, 38, 40, 41, 43, 44, 56, 57, 58, 59, 60, 80, 88, 89, 91, 95, 100, 101, 104, 105
Nel-O, 32

O

off, 22, 25, 27, 31, 42, 43, 44, 45, 46, 47, 48, 49, 55, 56, 57, 59, 60, 64, 65, 66, 67, 68, 69, 70, 71, 72, 73, 74, 75, 76, 77, 78, 81, 82, 84, 85, 99, 103, 104, 105
Opening Hand, 40, 63
Opening Hand Analysis, 40
options, 29, 33, 51
Order of Ranking, 23

P

Partners Strategies, 47
pips, 15, 16, 22, 23, 24, 27, 34, 60, 62, 99, 101, 103, 105
Playing a Game, 26
Plays, 67, 69, 78, 79, 81, 82, 83
Plunge, 32, 34, 44, 60, 89, 91, 95, 100, 105
points, 20
Preliminaries, 15
Protocol, 17, 104

R

Reneging, 17, 104
Round Robin, 88, 89
round', 14
rules sheet, 89

S

schedule, 88, 94
Score Status, 69
Scorecard 1 – Marks, 96
Scorecard 2 – Points, 97
Scoring, 20, 29, 30, 40, 95
Scoring and Winning, 20
set, 17, 18, 51, 105
Sevens, 29, 32, 34, 44, 60, 61, 62, 89, 95, 99, 100, 101, 105
shakes, 26, 90
shuffles, 26
Signaling', 18
Small End Lead, 23, 29, 31, 43, 55, 95
Splash, 32, 35, 44, 60, 89, 91, 95, 100, 105
stacked, 19, 21, 44, 89, 90, 91, 105
Strategy, 11, 33, 35, 37, 40, 44, 45, 51, 55, 63
suit, 14, 22, 23, 24, 25, 26, 27, 30, 31, 32, 33, 37, 41, 42, 43, 44, 46, 47, 50, 51, 52, 55, 56, 57, 58, 59, 60, 64, 66, 68, 69, 70, 71, 72, 73, 75, 76, 77, 78, 81, 82, 84, 89, 90, 91, 99, 101, 103, 104, 105

T

Table of Ranks, 23
team, 14, 15, 16, 17, 18, 19, 20, 22, 26, 27, 30, 31, 32, 33, 34, 37, 39, 40, 44, 45, 50, 51, 52, 53, 56, 57, 58, 59, 60, 62, 64, 66, 67, 68, 69, 70, 71, 75, 76, 77, 78, 79, 80, 81, 82, 84, 87, 88, 89, 90, 91, 92, 102, 104, 105
The Basic Game, 15
Timing, 74
T-n, 14
Tournament Play, 87
tournaments, 17, 87, 89, 102, 103
Tracking What Has Been Played That Is Important, 53
Tracking what has been played that matters, 51
Trappe Spring, 11
trick, 14, 16, 21, 24, 26, 27, 29, 30, 31, 32, 33, 34, 38, 42, 43, 44, 45, 46, 47, 48, 49, 50, 52, 53, 56, 57, 58, 59, 62, 63, 64, 65, 66, 67, 70, 71, 73, 74, 75, 76, 78, 79, 80, 81, 83, 84, 101, 103, 104, 105
Tricks, 15, 19, 21, 52

Tricks in play, 21
trump inventory, 45, 47, 51, 64, 82
Trump status, 69
Trump Status, 63, 70
Trump Void Hand, 51
Trumps, 14, 22, 23, 24, 25, 32, 53, 72, 74, 78, 82, 83, 101
Trumps and Leads, 22

V

Variations, 15, 27
Variations!, 5, 29

W

walkers, 17, 45, 47
Walkers Determination, 64
Walkers status, 69
Walkers Status, 73
Weatherford, 9, 12
When to play Count, 76
When to Play Offs, 76, 77
William Thomas, 11
Working your trumps, 79

Notes

CPSIA information can be obtained
at www.ICGtesting.com
Printed in the USA
BVHW02s0949110718
521088BV00031B/132/P